The Structure of Big History

The Structure of Big History

From the Big Bang until Today

FRED SPIER

AMSTERDAM UNIVERSITY PRESS

Cover illustration: Detail from "Afbeelding van 't Stadt Huys van Amsterdam", by Hubertus Quellinus (1661-1668).
Cover design: Marjan Wijsbeek, Pro Studio, Loosdrecht
Typesetting: Kronos Publishing Assistance, Amersfoort

ISBN 90 5356 220 6

© Fred Spier/Amsterdam University Press, Amsterdam, 1996

Contents

Preface and acknowledgments

At the University of Amsterdam, the sociologist Johan Goudsblom and myself, a biochemist, anthropologist and historical sociologist by training, are organising an interdepartmental course in what Australian historian David Christian calls "Big History". That is: an overview of all known history from the beginning of the Universe until life on Earth today.

Our curriculum has been modelled on the course *An Introduction to World History* set up by David Christian at Macquarie University, Sydney, Australia (see: Christian 1991). We have adapted his approach with the aid of our emerging sociological structuring principles, while revision of the contents has benefited from comments by contributing lecturers, whose specialities range from astronomy to the social sciences. While we have thought about and to some extent discussed the question of how to structure this summary of cosmic, planetary, world and human history for a number of years within our own circles, we have not yet written anything about it. Goudsblom has outlined some of his views on how to structure the history of humanity in *Human History and Social Process* (Goudsblom et al. 1989).

In this book, I will advance one single, all-encompassing, theoretical framework for big history. The need for such a scheme arose while considering how to integrate into our course portions of scientific knowledge that are usually widely separated. As a result of this specialisation, the various academic disciplines involved, ranging from astronomy to the social sciences, have all developed their own distinct theories, vocabularies and terminologies. And since very few people attempt to bring together all these forms of historical knowledge, the need for a single structuring scheme is rarely felt.

It is therefore not surprising that, as far as I know, no one before has suggested such an outline. However, we think we live in one single, undivided Universe, within one single Solar System, on one single planet, as one humankind, which, like all other living species, has descended from one single lifeform. In order to grasp this unity adequately, we need a type of unified knowledge that is not split along the fault lines of academic specialisations, which developed as part of our social history. If we wish to reach a comprehensive understanding of our big past, we must devise one single synthetic scheme that allows us to combine all existing theoretical and factual knowledge.

This is, of course, a most ambitious enterprise. It hardly needs saying that in no way do I claim to have written the final word in this respect. Because no scholarly tradition exists of designing "Grand Unified Theories of the Past", such schemes can only become established after a long and thorough academic discussion. In addition, in many disciplines, scientific knowledge is rapidly developing. This will almost inevitably lead to a need for rethinking this scheme somewhere in the future.

However, we live now, and must make do with our existing knowledge. As a result, my theoretical approach must be considered a first attempt at unifying sections of scientific historical knowledge that have grown apart for centuries, if not longer. I think the time is ripe for such an effort. In almost all branches of academic thought, the historical approach is gaining ground. We now have to devise an overarching scheme unifying all these historical approaches. I am not the only one who perceives such a need. The US world historian William H. McNeill, while commenting on our project, formulated it as follows: "the meeting of hard and soft sciences is much needed. It elevates history to the Queen of the Sciences: an interesting reversal from its status as a would-be science in the 19th century".

Whatever the reception of my proposal, for me, at least, the effort of producing the scheme presented in this book has contributed considerably to structuring our course in big history and, as a result, to structuring our approach to all of history itself.

This text is an improved and enlarged version of a paper presented at the 1995 Annual Conference of the World History Association in Florence, Italy. I have greatly profited from contributions to our course as well as from critical suggestions by astronomer Ed van den Heuvel, geologist Harry Priem, palaeobiochemist Peter Westbroek, palynologist and palaeoclimatologist Henry Hooghiemstra, biologist Frederick Schram, ethologist Adriaan Kortlandt, and archaeologist Jos Deeben. The world historians David Christian and William McNeill, ocean-ographer James Kennett, social scientists Wilma Aarts, Mart Bax, Ann Buckley, Johan Goudsblom, Johan Heilbron, Estellie Smith, Ruud Stokvis, Abram de Swaan, Nico Wilterdink, chemistry teacher Gijs Kalsbeek and biology student Filipa Vala provided valuable references, fascinating suggestions, critical comments and invaluable support for an enterprise that seemed impossible and hopelessly difficult when I first began thinking along these lines. David Christian, in particular, made many valuable sugges-tions and provided invaluable inspiration and support. Both David Christian and Alison Fisher corrected the English. Of course, I remain fully responsible for both the syntax and the con-tents.

I dedicate this book to Johan Goudsblom who, more than anyone else, has helped me to get on the track toward big history.

CHAPTER I

General approach

What is world history? So far, a compelling answer has eluded the World History Association. What the organization needs, a member remarked, is "a simple, all-encompassing, elegant idea" with the power to order all human experience.

Gilbert Allardyce in: 'Toward World History: American Historians and the Coming of the World History Course' (1990:67)

INTRODUCTION

I am not the first to address the question of how to structure the history of humanity. On the contrary: for centuries some of the best minds have struggled with this problem, and have produced a number of intriguing, illuminating but often controversial ideas, many of which now seem outdated.[1] Today, William McNeill, in particular, is emphasising the importance of, and interplay between, social and ecological aspects for the study of human history (1974-1995). The following analysis owes a great deal to his pioneering work.

Yet, with the exception of William McNeill and some other scholars such as Fernand Braudel, J.M. Roberts, Oswald Spengler, Leften Stavrianos, Arnold Toynbee (cf. Costello 1993), most historians employ structuring principles for (parts of) human history that remain more or less implicit in their writings, if they address the issue at all. By contrast, historical sociologists and anthropologists make use of explicit general schemes which can be illuminating, but which are sometimes not very suitable to accommodate all, or even most, of the established historical knowledge.[2] Also socio-biologists, geneticists in particular, have produced their own versions of world history.[3] Nowadays, the great majority of the historical profession as well as most sociologists and anthropologists refrain from taking the grand view.

1

As a result, the history of humanity still lacks a general paradigm, as David Christian recently formulated it. This is not, I think, because the history of our own species is too complicated and hence too difficult to grasp in a comprehensive theoretical manner, but rather because an established tradition of thinking in terms of human history does not yet exist. Consequently, we have as yet not made sufficient efforts to construct a suitable paradigm. In this context, it may be useful to emphasise that some other established branches of science, most notably cosmology and geology, have acquired their general paradigms only very recently.

Here, I do not aim to present an overview of current efforts to structure human history. Instead, I will make a rather big jump and advance one single, uncomplicated, conceptual scheme for all of history, of which human history is only a tiny part.

I will stretch my structuring design as far as possible and search for conceptualisations of a general kind which cover all of history, from the Big Bang, now accepted by most astronomers and cosmologists as the most likely explanation of the origin of the Universe, up to life on Earth today.[4] The outline presented here is not so much a theory that allows us to make experimental predictions or projections of the future. It is rather an intellectual framework that ought to facilitate ordering our knowledge in a hopefully disciplined way. It should also contribute to formulating research questions (and answers) of a different type and on an unusual scale.

This is a very ambitious enterprise. I suspect that some (or many) sceptical scholars may view this effort as an outdated nineteenth-century attempt destined to fail, as has happened with other efforts to set up similar grandiose schemes. But even if this argument fails, I hope it may provoke comments or ideas that stimulate further progress towards the construction of a unified paradigm for the study of the past on the very large scale.

REGIMES AS STRUCTURING ELEMENTS FOR COSMIC, PLANETARY AND HUMAN HISTORY

I propose to use the term 'regime' as the cornerstone of my structuring scheme for big history. I prefer the word 'regime' to terms such as system, order, pattern, constellation, configuration, field, etc. since 'regime' is the only term I know that can be utilised without hindrance to analyse all of big history. I will elaborate on this later. In my parlance, the term regime is identical to David Christian's "equilibrium systems". He described them as follows:

> In some sense history at all three levels [humanity, planet earth and the universe] is a fugue whose two major themes are entropy (which leads to imbalance, the decline of complex entities, and a sort of "running down" of the universe) and, as a sort of counterpoint, the creative forces that manage to form and sustain complex but temporary equilibria despite the pressures of entropy. These fragile equilibrium systems include galaxies, stars, the earth, the biosphere (what James Lovelock has referred to as "Gaia"), social structures of various kinds, living things and human beings. These are all entities that achieve a temporary but always precarious balance, undergo periodic crises, reestablish new equilibria, but eventually succumb to the larger forces of imbalance represented by the principle of "entropy" (1991:237).

I prefer the term regime to "equilibrium systems" because it is more flexible. In contrast to regimes, both 'systems' and 'equilibria' suggest more stability that can often be observed. As the above quotation illustrates, Christian is acutely aware of this, but his term may convey a different meaning to those who are not familiar with his underlying thoughts.

First of all, a few remarks about the history and daily use of the expression. The word regime comes from the Latin *regimen*, which in Roman antiquity meant both "guidance" and "rule" (Hanks et al. 1986:1286). In modern English, the meanings of *regime* and *regimen* include: a system of government, such as the regime of Fidel Castro; administration or rule; a social system or order; the set of conditions under which a system occurs or is maintained; a systematic course of therapy, or mode of living pertaining to health matters; the government of one word by another, the relation which one word in a sentence has to another word depending on it; the method of ordering and conducting anything, that it may answer its intentions, such as a regimen of fire use, a low voltage regime, and the working régime of a helicopter (Simpson and Weiner 1989:508, Hanks et al. 1986:1286).

In the 1980s, Dutch anthropologist Mart Bax and sociologist Abram de Swaan independently introduced the term regime into Dutch sociological discourse (cf. Bax 1982-1995, de Swaan 1982-1988). In the past ten years or so, the term regime has increasingly been used, especially within the emerging school of Dutch process sociology. This includes religious regimes (Bax), intellectual regimes (Heilbron 1995), medical regimes (de Swaan), educational regimes (de Vries 1993), regulatory regimes of intoxicants (Gerritsen 1993), ecological regimes including fire regimes (Goudsblom 1989, 1992), and assembly or meeting regimes (van Vree 1994).

While in worldwide sociological circles the use of the term regime is still a new phenomenon, in discussions among Anglo-Saxon political scientists the term "international regimes" has had great currency for more than a decade (Gupta et al. 1993, Haas 1980, 1989, Hayes & Smith 1993, Junne 1992, Krasner 1982, 1983, Young 1982, 1986, 1989a & b). Not all these regimes had international dimensions. As early as 1982, US political economist Oran Young wrote the illuminating book *Resource Regimes*, which claimed that such regimes operated at almost all levels of society.

However, Anglo-Saxon social scientists and historians refer to regimes rather sparingly, and when they employ the term, they do so in a rather offhanded fashion. Despite this, I have encountered "agricultural regimes" (Guillet 1983:563, Burger 1992:22), a "regimen of land-use" and a "regime of expanding worldwide markets" (McNeill 1978:3, 1994:9), a "garbage-disposal regime", the way people deal with refuse, as well as a "pig-slopping regime" (Rathje & Murphy 1992:92, 37), while in a recent lecture US social scientist James Scott spoke about "property", "tenure" and "labor regimes" (1995:9, 11, 23).

All these meanings refer to human behaviour. If we wish to make use of the term regime for all of history, this will inevitably imply widening its meaning. This journey has been made before by other terms such as energy, force and work, which were fully accepted within the natural sciences already long ago. I hope that the term regime will follow the example set by these respectable predecessors.

Before we set sail on this voyage, I will first discuss our sociological approach to human regimes. In so doing, I will depart from the most general modern common-sense meaning of the

4

term regime, namely "a social system or order". In our sociological usage, a regime is an interdependency constellation of all people who conform more or less to a certain social order.

HUMAN REGIMES

All human regimes are constellations of more or less institutionalised behaviour. In terms of the vocabulary developed by German sociologist Norbert Elias, regimes can be seen as patterns of constraint and self-restraint. In other words, they encompass comparatively stable patterns of things people feel they and others should do, and other things they feel the people involved should abstain from.

All human regimes appear to arise as a response to certain social, ecological and psychological problems. Johan Goudsblom has succinctly summarised this as follows (cf. 1977:137 ff., see also Spier 1994a). Living together creates problems. People continually seek to solve them, and in so doing, they create new ones.

The idea of human history as one continuous process of tackling problems and creating new ones is certainly not original. However, this notion is only rarely explored systematically, at least by historians. It is the most general interpretive scheme underlying our efforts at structuring human history. We cannot fully prove it, of course, since it is impossible to know all the motivations of all the people who have ever lived on this planet. But we think it is a plausible scheme, and as long as the existing evidence appears to fit and no better scheme is devised, we will stick to it.

Perhaps the most general statement we could make about the problems human beings are confronted with is that people always have to deal with themselves, with one another, and with the surrounding natural environment. Elias called this the "triad of basic controls" (1978a:156-157). This is so obvious as to seem completely trivial. While such an observation is very much to the point, it is only by starting the analysis at a very simple yet high level of abstraction that we can hope to erect a satisfactory, but still hopefully simple, framework which may help us to structure our common past.

5

Goudsblom has suggested using the general term 'social regime' for all rules and regulations that people observe to a greater or lesser extent in their dealings with each other (1994). Analogously, the term 'ecological regime' would indicate all more or less regulated behaviour people exhibit with regard to the rest of nature (Goudsblom 1989, 1992). In addition, I wish to introduce the term 'individual regime' to indicate all forms of control people exercise over themselves. This term bears a close resemblance to what Norbert Elias and the French sociologist Pierre Bourdieu have called 'habitus' (cf. Mennell 1989:30).

These three types of regimes are closely related to Elias's triad of basic controls. All human regimes can be seen as attempts at solving problems generated by our personal habitus, our socio-psychological and ecological make-up; problems originating from social life; and problems of how to relate to the non-human environment.[5]

Social, ecological and individual regimes never exist fully independently of each other. However, they can exhibit a certain degree of relative autonomy. For example, some people exercise forms of self-control that no one else demands from them. Their individual regimes can thus be relatively autonomous from the prevailing social or ecological regimes.

Social regimes must also be individual regimes but need not be ecological. For example, the ways in which we deal with etiquette are not necessarily associated with our relations with the surrounding natural environment. As a result, social regimes can be relatively autonomous with regard to ecological regimes. By contrast, all human ecological regimes are to some extent social regimes and are thus, by extension, all individual regimes. Consequently, a hierarchy of relative autonomy appears to exist between ecological, social and individual regimes. This curious hierarchy may have been overlooked until now. I do not wish to imply that ecological regimes determine all the other regimes. On the contrary, social and individual regimes can be relatively autonomous. Furthermore, they can, and very often do, influence the prevailing ecological regimes. As a result, a continuous interaction exists between the various regimes.

In order to avoid possible misunderstandings, it must be emphasised that people do not obey all existing forms of regulation to the same extent. Every rule, formal as well as informal, is violated at certain moments and to varying degrees. But even breaking the rules means some acknowledgment of them. The term regime thus indicates the existence of socially accepted or contested rules, and does not necessarily refer to all forms of behaviour, although in my view all behaviour can in principle be analysed in relation to the prevailing regimes.

All human regimes are to some extent intentional. I do not think, of course, that people always act fully consciously and intentionally. Their behaviour may have been internalised to such an extent that they follow many rules almost, or perhaps even completely, automatically. Yet intentions or consciousness are probably never completely absent in human behaviour. Emotions obviously play a large part, too, and such motivations are often not fully clear even to the people themselves (including myself). Some feelings, such as sexual attraction or repulsion, may have strong biological foundations. In other words, they are grounded in the human physiological regime. However, the ways in which people deal with their emotions and their biochemical constitution all form part of certain social regimes.

A short excursion into physical chemistry and quantum mechanics and a comparison with the type of theoretical approach advocated in those domains of science may be helpful to explain two related important traits of the term regime, namely its high level of generality and, as a result, its relative emptiness. This will also help to show that in many respects there are fewer conceptual differences and more similarities between the various branches of science than is often thought. Of course, in the natural sciences much more reliance is put on quantitative approaches, which can be pursued to far higher levels of abstraction than in biology or the social sciences. However, some general aspects and assumptions underlie all branches of science.

Back to the term regime in relation to the natural sciences. In the first part of this century, a number of European physicists devoted a great deal of attention to the question of how atoms stay together and thus form molecules. The problem was solved by the explanation that positively charged atomic nuclei are bonded by negatively charged electrons and, in so doing, can form molecular structures.

But how should all these movements and structures be described quantitatively? The most general answer to this question was formulated by the Austrian physicist Erwin Schrödinger in one single, rather simple-looking formula, since then known as the Schrödinger equation. It can be written down as follows:

$$\frac{d^2\psi}{dx^2} + \frac{d^2\psi}{dy^2} + \frac{d^2\psi}{dz^2} + \frac{8\psi^2 m}{h^2} (E - U)\psi = 0$$

(cf. Moore 1968:483)

What the terms mean is not of great importance here. I only want to underscore that this formula in principle describes all movements of all atomic nuclei and of all electrons, and thus provides a very general solution to a very general problem. However, as a result of this high level of abstraction and synthesis, the equation is rather empty. In order to describe even very uncomplicated molecular structures, such as an individual water molecule, the introduction of certain boundary conditions is needed. This is a simplification of reality and, as a consequence, strengthens the model character of the Schrödinger equation which is, in fact, already a model of reality.[6] And as soon as efforts are made to describe more complicated molecular structures, or even one nucleus with a greater number of surrounding electrons, the equation's theoretical constraints become even more severe.

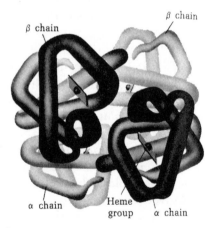

Fig. 1.1: *A molecular regime: the structure of the oxygen-transporting molecule haemoglobin (from: Lehninger 1975:146)*

The level of generality at which the Schrödinger equation has been formulated, which provides the basis for the description of all chemical bonds of all molecules, could set an example for the formulation of a truly general theory of human history, and also of big history. It is imperative to see that we need theories of this high level of generality, which can then be specified by introducing certain constraints or boundary conditions in order to describe actual life, according to the scale of the society we are seeking to understand as well as the time-span being examined.

I think that the term regime may well serve such a goal. The Schrödinger equation covers all regimes in the domain of micro-processes. This suggests that regimes should be seen as processes. They exist in time as well as space. Indeed, completely static regimes do not exist. The degree of change or stability of regimes is one of the major themes that need to be explored and explained. This is another reason why it is difficult to characterise regimes precisely.

In other words, the use of the word regime introduces a certain vagueness and openness. Regimes should not be reduced to neat timeless structures, nor can their limits be determined precisely. Regimes indicate arrays of possible fluctuations within certain limits that are hard to specify.

In this respect there is a remarkable similarity between the emerging sociology of regimes and quantum mechanics. According to the dominant modern view, the Schrödinger equation describes molecules as entities which cannot be precisely pinned down to rigid structures, but in which certain configurations are more probable than others. What is more, the chance that certain structures are repeated exactly is very small indeed. All this is characteristic of non-linear processes, which are omnipresent in nature, as chaos theoreticians emphasise (cf. Gleick 1988).

This fuzziness, also inherent in the term regime, may not be comforting to those who seek from science an elimination of all uncertainty. However, in my view it provides the best possible description of reality available at present. For an adequate analysis of fuzzy reality, we need fuzzy yet versatile concepts. Of course, such abstractions ought to fit into a consistent, systematic and hopefully simple theoretical framework. Just as today's electronic circuits based on fuzzy logic help to improve the functioning of electronic appliances of many kinds, fuzzy theoretical con-

9

cepts should facilitate the analysis of both society and inanimate nature.

Thus, in conclusion I would argue that precisely because of its relative vagueness and high level of generality, the term regime may be a useful analytical tool. It is for these reasons that I find the term 'regime' more attractive than other terms, such as system, configuration or constellation. All these suggest more precision than can actually be observed. In other words, the terms, and as a consequence the models associated with them, are in my view too rigid.

The vagueness of the term regime may be one of its greatest attractions, but it also makes it vulnerable to criticism. For how could the limits of a certain regime be defined, if they are vague by definition? In quantum mechanics, this problem is tackled mathematically. In principle, in that most formal branch of the natural sciences, the boundaries of a certain molecular regime can be delineated almost at will. This is usually done by formulating certain, comparatively arbitrary, constraints in terms of mathematical chance and probability. The limits of a molecule can, for instance, be defined by a chance of less than one per cent of finding any electrons beyond a certain distance from the nucleus.

This approach indicates how I will tackle this problem. Although in many cases, especially in biology and the social sciences, we do not have mathematical calculations at our disposal that could help us to set limits with similar precision, the strategy could be used to define certain arbitrary boundaries on which most people would agree. While this strategy could work in principle, in the everyday world of academe it will probably face considerable resistance. Regrettably, especially in the social sciences, it seems unlikely that a general agreement on anything can be achieved today.

For instance, a Catholic regime, those people who to some degree adhere to certain Catholic ideas and behaviourial standards, could be defined with the aid of the self-definition of all persons involved, all the people who describe themselves as Catholic. In contrast, from a clerical point of view, only those who had passed through certain rituals and were obeying certain clerically approved standards of belief and conduct would be included. And to complicate the analysis, while it is more likely than not that even in one particular period clerical agreement on

10

such matters did not exist, I suspect that priestly opinions also have varied in the course of time (cf. Spier 1994b). Thus, the limits of such a regime can only be determined by the academics who study them, and will always involve some arbitrariness. Of course, reality places some constraints on the degree of scholarly subjectivity.

Fig. 1.2: *Benediction of a warrior, part of the Catholic regime (from: Picard 1723:115)*

On the larger scale of the surrounding physical world we encounter the same problem. Where, for instance, are the limits of our Solar System? Nowadays, it is increasingly recognised that beyond Pluto, as far as we know the planet farthest removed from the Sun, countless small chunks of matter are circling our central star. These are now collectively known as the Kuiper Belt in honour of Dutch-born US astronomer Gerard Kuiper (Hecht 1994, 1995b:19). No one knows how many such meteoroids and dirty snowballs there may be, and how far removed they are from the Sun. So, where are the limits of our 'solar regime'? No one would leave out Pluto or the giant planets Uranus and Neptune, although they are invisible to the naked eye. Thus, the limits of our 'solar regime' should be drawn beyond the outer planets, but where?

The Sun is emitting a constant stream of high-energy particles collectively called solar wind. Some scientists argue that the limits of the Solar System have been reached when we can no longer measure this particle stream. Currently, a few planetary spacecraft are en route to leave the Solar System. They are still sending data back to Earth, including measurements of solar wind, which could help determine the edge of the Solar System. However, by following this approach, we define the solar regime in terms of the lower limits of what we can measure now, which is, in my view, just as arbitrary as all the other definitions. Again, only by imposing to some extent subjective boundary conditions can we solve this problem.

Thus, like all ordering concepts and structuring principles, the limits of regimes and, as a consequence, the precision of the term depend on the choices made by intelligent and sensitive academics, and will always be controversial to some extent. In this context, it is important to underscore that regimes are analytic and didactic models, the best possible representations of reality, maps of reality in a sense, but not reality itself.

In any regime, the parts make up the 'whole', but the 'whole' is more than sum of the parts. In other words, regimes define higher levels of complexity. All these higher levels can be said to have some relative autonomy with respect to all the lower levels. This simply means that more complex (and thus less general) regimes cannot be adequately explained by a theory pertaining to 'lower' levels of complexity. This includes atomic and molecular regimes. From a scientific point of view, for instance, even chemistry cannot completely be reduced to quantum physics (cf. Primus 1985a & b).[7]

The last general observation I wish to make is that all of nature can be viewed as regimes. After what I have said so far, this is perhaps no longer surprising. But what is more, I think that there is no regime-less nature. This may be less obvious. In my view, there are also regimes to be found in the at first sight chaotic and chance behaviour of a great many situations, such as that of air molecules in our atmosphere or of water molecules in the oceans. I view them as part of larger regimes, namely the oceans and the atmosphere as a whole. Even the relative vacuum of extra-galactic space exists within the regime of the Universe as a whole. Thus, while chance and chaos obviously do exist and are attract-

12

ing growing attention particularly within the natural sciences, no completely unstructured part of nature exists.

This also implies that any definition of chaotic behaviour depends on the scale of inquiry. Phenomena which at a lower level of analysis appear to be chaotic may display more order when viewed from a higher, more all-embracing perspective.

INORGANIC REGIMES

The comparison between intentional human regimes and molecular structures suggests how the concept of regime can be stretched from the human world to non-human biological and physical nature, both at the very small scale level of atoms and molecules and at the very large scale of the Universe as a whole, as well as everything in between. In fact, human history can be viewed as caught between physical micro- and macroprocesses (cf. Morrison & Morrison 1994).

This has, to my knowledge, not yet been discussed systematically in terms of regimes. As I mentioned earlier, in academic texts as well as in daily usage, references to human regimes are on the increase. However, even non-human regimes are beginning to crop up now and then in the Anglo-Saxon academic literature, most notably in environmental studies. For example, British geographer I.G. Simmons loosely referred to a changing "water regime" when a certain area was deforested (1993:5). Elsewhere, I have encountered a riverine "flood regime" (Ben-Tor 1992:17) as well as a "sedimentary regime" (Vrba 1993:405). This is in line with another well-established way of using the term regime. Already in the nineteenth century, a river regime was an accepted expression, while later regimes of lakes, sandbanks and glaciers appeared, including a theory of canal regimes. In addition, both a "pluvial régime" and a "régime of desiccation" have been mentioned (Simpson & Weiner 1989:508). On a grander scale, there is thought to be a "régime of eastward winds and currents" of the eastern Pacific Ocean (Ronan & Needham 1986:157), while the more general term "climate" or "climatic regime" can be found in several studies (Cohen 1977:265, Lovelock 1987:24, Redman 1978:233, Stanley & Warne 1993:438, Wilson 1994:259). At a more general level, British geographer Neil Roberts mentioned

13

and biological regimes" in combination with "cultural
)89:92).

o life at the microlevel has been described with the term
According to US biologist and computer scientist Stuart
Kaufman, "the genomic networks that control development from
zygote to adult can exist in three major regimes: a frozen ordered
regime, a gaseous chaotic regime, and a kind of liquid regime
located in the region between order and chaos" (1995:26). In their
book *Atmosphere, Climate and Change*, US natural scientist Thomas
Graedel and Dutch Nobel-prize winner, chemist Paul Crutzen,
provided a definition of the term 'system' which is almost indis-
tinguishable from my regime approach (1995:2). However, on the
very next page they mentioned "five different Earth system
regimes with widely varying impacts and timescales", namely the
"atmosphere, the biosphere, the hydrosphere, the cryosphere and
the pedosphere" (1995:3). In their discussion of non-equilibrium
thermodynamics, the Belgian physicists Nobel laureate Ilya Prigogine and Isabelle Stengers referred to a "new regime" of unstable natural systems on a very small scale (1984:141), while closer
to the other extreme, the regimes of intense pressure and high
temperatures of the interior of the Sun (Trefil 1989:95) and the
more general term "celestial regime" (Morrison & Morrison
1994:5) have already been coined.

These examples indicate the way in which I will employ the
term regime for analysing big history. I define a regime in its most
general sense as: "a more or less regular but ultimately unstable
pattern that has a certain temporal permanence". This is a pretty
vague definition. I do so on purpose, of course, since I am seeking a term that is as general and empty as possible while still hav-
ing the capacity to focus attention in a way I find useful. This definition includes human cultural regimes, human and non-human
physiological regimes, non-human nature, as well as all organic
and inorganic nature at all levels of complexity. By defining
regimes in this way, human cultural regimes become a sub-cat-
egory of regimes in general. It is of paramount importance to see
that in contrast to human cultural regimes, all inanimate regimes,
and perhaps the great majority of biological regimes as well, are
formed and maintained through unconscious, unintentional
interactions.

CHAPTER II

Human life between micro and macro regimes

INTRODUCTION

At the elementary level of microprocesses, interactions at atomic and subatomic levels as well as the great variety of molecular structures can all be viewed as sets of regimes that are operating according to the rules of what are now regarded as the four (or perhaps three) basic forces: the large and weak forces, electromagnetism and gravity. All larger structures, inorganic as well as organic (ranging from molecules to the entire Universe), are built upon, and are thus relatively dependent on, these basic atomic and molecular regimes.

As US physicist Nobel laureate Leon Lederman and astrophysicist David Schramm put it: "The two stories of inner space and outer space came together in the 1980s in a most dramatic way" (1995:i). The dominant explanations of the origin of the Universe, Big Bang cosmology, and of the origins of the tiniest building blocks of matter, elementary physics, have now merged into one coherent historical processual narrative to an extent unimaginable until recently (see also: Barrow 1994, Gribbin 1993, Longair 1996, Reeves 1981, Silk 1994, Weinberg 1993).

The search for a 'theory of everything' fusing the basic forces into one single paradigm continues to attract a great deal of attention. However, whatever the outcome of this enterprise, it is certain that any unified theory of micro- and macroprocesses will not explain everything, as Dutch physicist Frans Saris often emphasises (1995). All the intermediate levels of complexity, ranging from molecular to astronomical regimes, are relatively autonomous, and thus need relatively autonomous explanatory theories.

In this chapter, I will elaborate a conceptional scheme that does justice to the relative autonomy of such theories and yet provides an overarching framework that makes it possible to merge them into 'one unified theory of the past'. I will mostly concentrate on our planetary regime and on human life as taking place between micro and macro regimes. This is, of course, a rather earth- and anthropocentric approach. However, apart from pleasing our perhaps inborn self-interest, this hopefully illustrates how the interactions between all these different levels of complexity can be looked at in a rather simple manner.

ASTRONOMICAL REGIMES

I propose to use the term 'astronomical regime' as a general term for the analysis of the Universe as a whole. This would include the 'solar regime', a term I used above to indicate some of the recurrent patterns exhibited by our Solar System. But there are more intriguing regularities to be observed. For instance, in 1766 Prussian astronomer Johann Titius observed that all then known planets were removed from each other at more or less regular distances. This idea, soon known as the Titius-Bode law, "got a major boost in 1781 with the discovery of Uranus" and contributed to locating Neptune in 1846 (Matthews 1994:13). In 1994, two French astronomers, François Graner and Bérengére Dubrulle, would have claimed that "such a 'law' is a natural consequence of certain symmetry properties, some of which are almost certain to feature in any planetary system" (ibid.). In addition, the four inner planets are all of similar size, small compared with the outer planets. All inner planets have a solid crust, while all the known outer planets are gas giants with the exception of Pluto, whose origins are unclear (Reeves 1981, Gribbin 1993, Murray 1989).

Furthermore, it is increasingly recognised that the orbits of all the planets continually influence one another and, by doing so, produce a pattern characteristic of non-linear, or chaotic, processes (cf. Gleick 1988, Peterson 1995). In the popular view based on classical Newtonian physics, the orbits of the planets around the Sun were viewed as repetitious and virtually identical. However, for about three centuries astronomers and mathematicians have wrestled with the undeniable fact that no single orbit of any planetary object is completely identical to its predecessors, nor will it be identical to any of its successors. This is so, because the movement of the Earth around the Sun is influenced by the other planets, which travel with different velocities than the Earth. This argument applies to all interactions between all of the objects that make up the Solar System. As a result, although for a long time the planets appear to have moved around the Sun within rather narrow boundaries and probably will continue to do so for a long time to come, every configuration of the planets around the Sun at any given moment is unique. From their unique positions, all the planets influence each other and continue to produce new unique configurations. This is the regime of the Solar System in which we live.[1]

Although measurable, for common purposes the differences between successive planetary orbits are negligible. Yet one may marvel at the fact that for as long as we can tell, the orbits of the planets have shifted between these rather narrow limits. They have a certain bandwidth, to borrow a phrase from the world of radio. I propose to describe this situation as a rather stable astronomical regime of limited size.

This has important implications for the earthly planetary regime. For instance, the orbit of the Earth around the Sun may be shifting back and forth from a more elliptical to a more circular form at regular intervals lasting about 100,000 years. Also, the angle between the Earth's axis and the plane of its orbit around the Sun periodically varies slightly on a comparable timescale. The precession of the Earth's axis is another regular astronomical pattern of similar time-span. All these movements are jointly called Milankovitch cycles, in honour of the Yugoslav mathematician who elaborated the idea that these astronomical changes would be related to climate change on Earth (van Andel 1994:90-94).

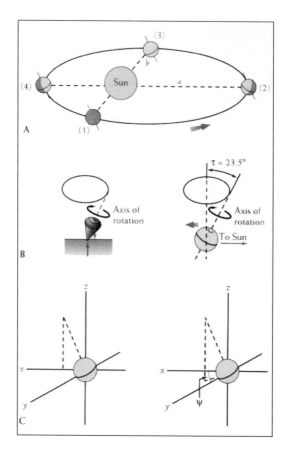

Fig. 2.1: *The Milankovitch cycles: shifts in the earthly astronomical regime of eccentricity, precession and tilt (from: Graedel & Crutzen 1995:76)*

Since then, evidence has been accumulating that an intricate interplay exists between these patterns, which indeed appear to contribute to periodic climate shifts. This, in turn, may accelerate biological evolutionary changes, including the evolution of early hominids some 2.5 million years ago. In that period, as a result of the Milankovitch cycles worldwide climate change took place. In Central Africa, forested areas declined, making way for savanna lands. The forest-dwelling species found themselves increasingly under pressure to adapt to life on these grasslands, which led to a growing speciation, not only among early hominids (or apes) but also among antelopes and other herbivores (van

18

Andel 1994:90-94, Gamble 1995:79-84, Tudge 1993, Vrba 1993, Vrba et al. 1996). I would describe this situation as a dominant astronomical regime which influences the earthly climatic regime which, in its turn, dominates the biological regime.

Plate tectonics, part of the earthly geological regime, may also have played a dominant part in driving biological evolution, including early human evolution. Continuous shifts in the positions of the Earth's land masses led, among other things, to changes in ocean currents which, in turn, influenced the global climate. Continental uplift and mountain formation altered wind and rain patterns everywhere on Earth. In the same period as climatic change was inducing a shift from woodlands to savannas, an ecological 'barrier' developed as a result of plate tectonics, linking the Nile, Rift, and Zambezi valleys, thereby to some extent separating eastern from western Africa. In the course of time this will lead to the break-up of the African continent. Although a great many species could, and can, cross this boundary without any great problems and thus remained part of one single gene pool, some others could not.

According to Dutch ethologist Adriaan Kortlandt, this emerging ecological barrier prevented early hominids (or apes) on both sides from interbreeding, since presumably they could not swim and thus were unable to cross the rivers that developed in these valleys. As the ecological circumstances began to vary to the east and west of the barrier, so did biological evolution, so that in the forests of West Africa chimpanzees emerged, while on the savannas to the east of the Rift valley early humans began to develop (Kortlandt 1972, see also: Coppens 1994 and Kortlandt vs. Coppens 1994). In general terms, I see this as an example of how dominant geological and climate regimes can influence human evolution.

The rise of early states may also have been connected to such larger influences. Recently, US archaeologist Douglas Kennett and his father, oceanographer James Kennett, have advanced the following hypothesis linking astronomical, climatic and human cultural regimes in the same order of dominance (1994). Rising sea levels after the last ice age led to the inundation of what then became the Arabo/Persian Gulf. As the sea level first rose steeply and then slightly dropped, the coastline retreated inland very rapidly. On sites where the coastline had receded the farthest, the remains of the oldest known cities of that region have been found. These are considered the earliest city-states in human history. The central idea is that the decreasing area suitable for human life led to an increasing concentration of people in places where habitation remained possible. This resulted in growing competition, which may have contributed to the rise of 'civilisation'. I will elaborate this argument later when exploring early state formation in terms of regimes.

There may be more astronomical regimes in operation within our Solar System. After the spectacular collision of the comet Shoemaker-Levy with the giant planet Jupiter in July 1994, astronomers began to wonder whether Jupiter may act as a comet catcher, and thus protect the Earth to some extent against such disasters. According to US astronomer and computer modeller George Wetherill, "the earth would suffer catastrophic impacts about once every 100 000 years instead of once in 100 million years if Jupiter were not around" (quoted by Hecht 1995a:14, see also: Croswell 1992:18). It is now increasingly recognised that large impacts of celestial bodies on Earth seem to occur more or less regularly, and may therefore be seen as part of an astronomical regime.

Jupiter may not only exercise a beneficial influence on life on this planet, but may also be a root cause of periodic meteoroid impacts on Earth. Currently, it is thought that at more or less regular intervals, chunks of the asteroid belt, situated between the inner and outer planets,[2] leave their orbits under the influence of gravitational forces from Jupiter and become stray objects within our Solar System. When they collide with the Earth, the planetary organic and inorganic regimes are upset. This may produce significant changes in the biological regime. The situation could be described as an interaction between a dominant astronomical regime and a dominated earthly climatic regime, contributing to mass extinctions and a "punctuated equilibrium" type of evolution (cf. Gould 1993, 1994, Raup 1993, Wilson 1994).

In this process, regimes between species large and small may shift as a result of changes in ecological niches, or in the occupation of them by different species. For instance, the famous extinction of the dinosaurs about 65 million years ago, now increasingly explained as a result of a large asteroid impact, may well have provided the opportunity for mammals to spread. Changes in the biological regime as a result of more or less regular astronomical influences may, therefore, have been an important driving force of evolution (cf. Gould 1989, 1993, 1994).

One could even speculate on the question of how the particular shape of our solar regime may have contributed to the formation and development of life on Earth. For instance, US astronomer and computer scientist Jacques Laskar has recently concluded from his calculations modelling the Solar System that:

> if the [orbits of] the outer planets were less regular, then the inner planets' motion would be so chaotic that...Earth would suffer changes too large in its orbit to ensure climatic stability on its surface (quoted in: Peterson 1995:270).

Thus, the configuration of the solar regime as a whole may have been vital for allowing life to develop on this planet. It is as yet unclear to what extent our Solar System is unique, or whether this configuration is common throughout the Universe. For lack of sufficient knowledge I will therefore not explore this theme any further.

I wish to advance an even more unsubstantiated hypothesis, namely that the interactions of solar systems within galaxies, of galaxies forming larger clusters, and perhaps even of clusters of galaxies making up even larger structures, may all be considered regimes, which would entail certain consequences for the parts that make up the wholes. I do not know what these consequences would be, but perhaps astronomers will come forward with some suggestions.

The very large-scale view of the past proposed here immediately suggests the possibility that regimes at the scale of solar systems should be seen as relatively autonomous elements of even larger galactic regimes which, in turn, belong to even larger regimes at the level of galactic clusters. Stars, for instance, do not originate on their own at random. Their formation always takes place within larger structures. The same applies to planets and moons, and even to galaxies. A variety of interactions between astronomical regimes at various scales appears to contribute to the emergence of these structures. Explanations at all these different levels may well be improved by a greater sensitivity to the way in which regimes are embedded in other regimes.

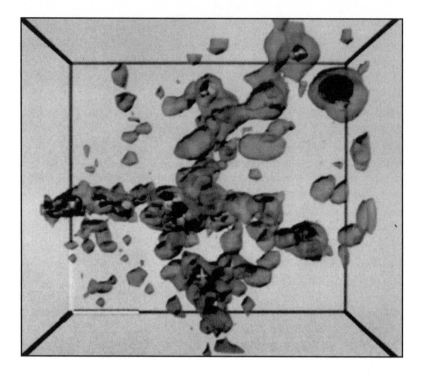

Fig. 2.2: *A galactic regime: the Local Supercluster of galaxies (from: Krisciunas
& Yenne 1989:180)*

To summarise and place this discussion within the context of big
history: seen from a very long-term perspective, the origins of the
Universe and of our Galaxy and Solar System could be described
as the development of particular types of astronomical regimes.
According to the current standard cosmological view, on a certain
moment all the matter and energy of the Universe was closely
packed together in one single regime. No one knows what happened before that moment. But it seems that from that time, matter and energy began to spread and take shape. In the process, the
first-known regime differentiation began, which is still continuing today. At about 300,000 years after the Big Bang, the regimes
of matter and energy separated from each other, and the Universe
as a whole became 'transparent'. This is the moment at which the
cosmic background radiation, first detected in 1964, was generated. The first elementary particles began to form, and later elements and molecules. Galaxies, stars and other bodies of many

different shapes started to coalesce and influence one another. In
a long process of internal development and decay of such bodies

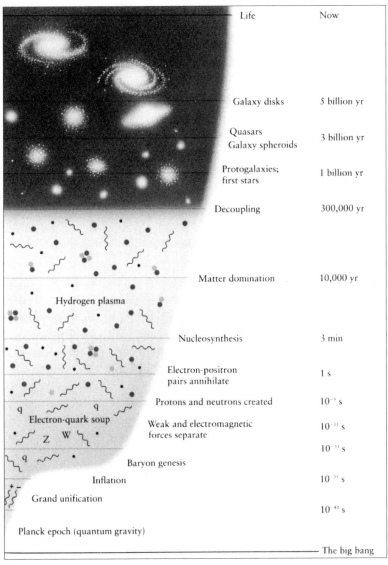

	Life	Now
	Galaxy disks	5 billion yr
	Quasars Galaxy spheroids	3 billion yr
	Protogalaxies; first stars	1 billion yr
	Decoupling	300,000 yr
	Matter domination	10,000 yr
Hydrogen plasma		
	Nucleosynthesis	3 min
	Electron-positron pairs annihilate	1 s
	Protons and neutrons created	10^{-5} s
Electron-quark soup	Weak and electromagnetic forces separate	10^{-11} s
		10^{-11} s
	Baryon genesis	
	Inflation	10^{-36} s
Grand unification		10^{-43} s
Planck epoch (quantum gravity)		
		The big bang

Fig. 2.3: *Regime differentiation in the history of the Universe (from: Silk
1994:87)*

as well as of their mutual interactions, the present Universe came into being, of which our solar regime is only a very tiny part.

On the early Earth, when life did not yet exist, a type of inorganic regime developed when the Earth's crust formed, plate tectonics began, and the atmosphere first took shape. All these various interactions must have exhibited some regularities, all of which could be summarised by the term 'planetary inorganic regime'.

ORGANIC AND BIOLOGICAL REGIMES

According to the modern view, before life began to develop, organic molecules of various sorts formed. The term 'organic' can be misleading. It suggests that all such molecules have a relation to living organisms, or rather, have been produced by them. For the great majority of existing organic matter, this is the case, which explains the name of the category. However, modern chemistry defines molecules as organic when they are composed of a certain type of bonding (covalent bonds) between at least one carbon atom and some others. Many of these molecules of novel design are being synthesised in chemical laboratories and factories at a growing rate and in increasing quantities.

However, even before any life existed on this planet organic molecules were synthesised in the great laboratory of the primordial earth, perhaps mainly under the influence of volcanism (oceanic in particular), solar light and lightning. No one knows to what extent and in what variety such organic molecules existed, but there is a consensus that they formed the environment that was essential for the early development of life. In other words, in the initial history of the Earth an organic regime must have arisen which, in all likelihood, not only changed over the course of time but also varied from place to place.

The composition of this "primordial soup" is one of the hotly debated topics of modern palaeochemistry. This is not the place to enter into this discussion. But one aspect needs to be underscored. Before life, there were no organisms that could take up, adapt or destroy organic molecules. As a result, the pre-life organic regime must have been fundamentally different from that after life established itself. This aspect becomes clear when considering that as far as we know until very recently, up until modern efforts began to synthesise organic molecules, all organic matter formed part of one or more life cycles. In other words, life must have consumed the primordial soup completely. In terms of regimes: the regimes of living organisms will strongly have influenced the general organic regime and had, in fact, incorporated all aspects of it until modern chemists appeared on the planetary stage.

It is unknown how life first took shape. The fact that the genetic code of all living organisms is similar strongly suggests one common ancestry. Some scientists argue that life was introduced from outer space by meteoroids or whatever things happened to fall on early Earth and survive the impact sufficiently to introduce the life-forms that travelled with them into the new planetary surroundings.

Others think that processes of self-organisation leading to life took place spontaneously. In his ground-breaking analysis, Stuart Kauffman has recently suggested that simple organising principles may operate in such processes, bringing about life and sets of life-forms as an almost inevitable consequence of growing molecular complexity and diversity (1995). After spontaneous self-organisation had begun generating the first living things – which are simply complex molecular regimes able to reproduce themselves –, Darwin's mechanism of natural selection would have started acting as a filter, allowing fitter organisms to produce more, and/or more efficient, offspring than others. The best-adapted organisms appear to be those which are neither too rigid to adapt to change nor too chaotic to fall apart as soon as conditions alter. In order to optimise their chances for survival, living things need to be somewhere in between those extremes. Kauffman formulated his hypothesis as follows:

> It is as though a position near the transition to chaos affords the best mixture of stability and flexibility (1995:91). *The reason complex systems exist on, or in the ordered regime near, the edge of chaos is because evolution takes them there* (1995:90, his emphasis).[3]

I think that some of the principles Kauffman sees behind the growing complexity and self-organisation of life may also be applicable to the emergence of inanimate regimes, ranging from the formation of galaxies to many kinds of molecular assemblies. In all of these cases, spontaneous regime formation takes place, defying the forces of entropy that are supposed to destroy all thermodynamically unstable order. Of course, this can only happen when there is an energy source of some sort which assists in countering entropy, thus providing the essential preconditions for the formation of complexity. In the case of life on Earth, the primary energy sources are sunlight and heat emanating from the Earth's interior generated by nuclear decay and gravitational pressure. Kauffman's ideas suggest a very promising line of inquiry that urgently needs to be explored.

Whatever the case turns out to be, when life began to develop, the earthly inorganic and organic regimes as a whole became supplemented by the various mutually interacting biological regimes developing side by side. It is, however, of overriding importance to see that all biological regimes were influenced by, and also influenced, the organic and inorganic regimes on Earth (cf. for instance: Gould 1993, Lovelock 1987, Priem 1993, Westbroek 1992). All these interactions between different regimes were summarised by British scientist James Lovelock in his "Gaia hypothesis", while other earth scientists speak about "System Earth" (cf. Priem 1993). It is not yet very clear how these interdependencies should be described, or how the balances are tilted.

The successive colonisation of ever greater parts of the globe by increasing numbers of species led to ever more complex relations between and among the various regimes of living things, as well as to a growing interplay between them and the planetary organic and inorganic regimes (cf. Westbroek 1992). For instance, plants keep soil together, and thus change erosion patterns. Conversely, certain mosses and bacteria 'eat' rock, and thus speed up other types of erosion. Calcium-binding single-cell organisms such as *Emiliania*, living in the oceans in great numbers, intervene in the carbon cycle and help to cause the formation of rain clouds. After they die and sink to the bottom of the sea, their calcium carbonate-rich shells form sediments on the ocean floor. From these deposits, limestone rocks originate through the process of plate tectonics.

Life's colonisation of the landmasses could only take place after photosynthesis by blue and green algae (and later by plants) had begun. This removed ever greater amounts of carbon dioxide from the atmosphere and replaced it with free oxygen. As a further consequence, the stratospheric ozone layer was formed, which began shielding the Earth from solar ultraviolet rays. It was only after this aspect of the atmospheric regime had developed that living things could start invading the land. Before that time, sea water protected them against damage caused by sunlight.

As a result of the ever-continuing movements of the Earth's crust because of plate tectonics, in the course of many millions of years most of the atmospheric carbon was enwrapped in sediments and could no longer take part in any life cycles. Both organic and inorganic carbon in various forms sedimented to the ocean floors, and were subsequently locked away deep beneath the Earth's surface through the mechanism of plate tectonics. This allowed for the continuity of an oxygen-rich atmosphere on which all higher animal life depends. Therefore, both the biological and the inanimate geological regimes make a critical contribution to the planetary regime as a whole in a process of continuous mutual interaction. In the words of Dutch palaeo-biochemist Peter Westbroek:

> It is the combined effects of the biological cycle and the rock cycle that have made the global system. The biological cycle fuels the battery. The internal mechanism of the planet maintains the rock cycle, buries the organic matter, and sets the oxygen free. Without plate tectonics we would not be here (1992:201).

Thus, the emergence and development of the biological regime strongly influenced the general planetary regime (and vice versa), thereby creating at least some of the conditions for its own continuity and development.

The interplay between all these earthly regimes was influenced by various astronomical regimes, the shifting parameters of the earthly astronomical regime and, most spectacularly, by the impacts of celestial bodies on Earth, but not the other way around, I would suspect. On the very small scale, the atomic and molecular regimes posed clear limits on the development of higher levels of earthly complexity. However, the emergence of life influenced and created molecular structures that had not existed hitherto. Life and the microprocesses of atomic and mol-

27

ecular structures thus interacted mutually, although in different ways. As we have seen, the development of life also began to influence the planetary regime. Within the biological regime as a whole, mutual interactions became the rule.

In all these examples one general principle can be discerned: that of continuously interacting regimes. The influences of one regime on the other and vice versa can be seen as balances of influence. When both regimes influence one another to more or less the same extent, the balance is rather even. By contrast, when one regime influences the other but not vice versa, the first regime is fully dominant. In most cases, however, the balance between different regimes is somewhere between those two extremes. Seen from a long-term perspective, all these balances are unstable, although to a varying extent, also depending on the time-span. Here we can observe a criterion that is of paramount importance for the structuring of big history, the shifts in balances of influence between the various regimes.

A second general principle is that regimes do not merely interact; they come into being, flourish (not always to the same extent, of course), and eventually disintegrate. Regimes never rise from nothing. They always separate from already-existing regimes. This is true for regimes of all dimensions, with the exception perhaps of the Universe as a whole. We simply do not know whether the Universe is part of an even larger regime. The formation and development of regimes can only take place when there is some amount of instability in the 'parent regime', but not too much, of course, since otherwise the 'parent regime' would not have existed. The breakdown of a regime is the result of too much instability, generated from within the regime itself, introduced through outside interference, or both. In the words of David Christian:

> They ['equilibrium systems'] all share the rhythm of "punctuated equilibrium" that Stephen Jay Gould and Niles Eldredge have detected in the history of life on earth. These are entities that live, develop, and then die. Such patterns can be found at all time scales, so in this sense history is, as the mathematicians of chaos would say, "self-similar." Seen in this perspective, human history is the story of one such equilibrium system, which exists on the scale of a million or so years (1991:237-238).

28

The appearance, development or disappearance of a particular regime can have profound effects on other, related regimes. This applies to the explosion of a star at the end of its regular life cycle as much as to the extinction of a biological species.

With the development of more complex organisms, plants and animals in particular, a further regime differentiation among and within species began to take shape. Also, one single representative of any multicellular species can be seen as a regime, whereby the whole is more than the sum of its parts. When cells were becoming specialised, increasing mutual coordination (and thus communication) between and among them was needed to prevent the regime from disintegrating. The formation of specialised organs, such as in the case of our own species a brain, lungs, etc., can be viewed as a further regime differentiation within a single organism.

The relations of biological regimes between and among species can represent the entire spectrum from mutually threatening, competing, indifferent, to supportive. All animals and many bacteria feed on other species. One of the central problems of all individuals of any species is finding food while avoiding becoming food (cf. McNeill 1985:13). This is not competition for the same ecological niche, but simply a struggle for survival. In other instances, the regimes represented by different species as well as individuals within a single species do compete with one another for (parts of) the same ecological niche. This led to what Darwin called the process of natural selection.

Threats to survival may also have come about without any direct interaction between species, simply because certain organisms influenced the general biological regime in ways that were beneficial to some and harmful to others. For instance, as I mentioned earlier, the onset of photosynthesis through the action of algae led to growing amounts of free oxygen in the atmosphere, which poisoned many existing micro-organisms or at least drove them to a marginal existence deep in the oceans or underground (Lovelock 1987:29-31, Sepkoski in: Gould 1993:44, Westbroek 1992:200-202). At the same time, the creation of an oxygen-rich atmosphere entailed, of course, great benefits to some other species. From then on, organisms could begin to stoke their life cycle by burning organic material with the aid of atmospheric oxygen. Thus, free oxygen in the air drove some species to the deepest depths of the biosphere, while it allowed others to colonise the highest mountains on Earth.

According to a recent report (Flanagan 1995:17), another spectacular example of indirect harm was presented by the series of massive marine extinctions that took place between 382 million and 362 million years ago, collectively known as the late Devonian crisis. "At least 70 per cent of all marine species were wiped out in what was a very selective crisis, killing off many tropical bottom dwelling animals, such as corals and other reef organisms, while leaving many high-latitude species unharmed." A team led by US biologist Thomas Algeo has suggested that this was caused by the establishment of plant life on land. Ruth Flanagan summarised Algeo's position as follows:

> As root-bearing plants first began to colonise previously barren areas, their initial effect would have been to break up the surface both chemically and physically, making it more susceptible to weathering and erosion. The emergence of trees, in particular, would have had a dramatic effect as their large root systems descended into the ground and started to break up rocks. By rendering soils more susceptible to weathering and erosion, Algeo argues, the burgeoning populations of Devonian plants caused large amounts of soil particles and nutrients to be washed into rivers and oceans. The nutrients fertilised the waters, he argues, causing an explosive growth of algae. As these algae died, their decomposition would have used up the oxygen from the ocean's deep layers, suffocating many marine animals.

Of course, this is still a largely unconfirmed hypothesis. Whatever the merits of this idea will prove to be, I would not be surprised if many less severe cases are found in most, if not all, aspects of the planetary biological regime. In all likelihood, we need to view the earthly ecosystem not only as making life in general possible by creating and sustaining the proper conditions, but also as continuously threatening the survival of particular species through such indirect influences.

In addition, quite often species do exist close together without either competing or supporting one another. Although, in my view, the existence of neutral forms of mutual behaviour needs to be explained, too, this rather unspectacular subject does not

30

appear to have received a great deal of scholarly attention. The forms of mutually benefiting cohabitation by plants and bacteria, humans and bacteria and, more recently, between people and domesticated plants, animals and micro-organisms, have received a great deal of academic attention. These could also be seen as specific socio-ecological regimes, depending on the point of view.

As far as we know, most of these processes of biological, organic and inorganic regime formation, differentiation, continuation, decline and eclipse are unconscious. All inorganic and non-living organic regime formation and development must, by definition, be insensate. In the realm of biological regimes, it is very difficult to determine precisely where consciousness begins. I would suspect that many animal species exhibit some forms of conscious behaviour, but this question is very difficult to tackle, and general agreement about it is lacking. But even if consciousness does not exist, in many cases learning certainly does, even for very small organisms.

Although in the preceding sections I have only traced a first outline of the interplay between all the various regimes ranging from astronomical via biological to molecular and atomic dimensions, I will not explore these themes any further here, but will now concentrate on human cultural regimes in relation to the other regimes.

CHAPTER III

Human cultural regimes

INTRODUCTION

From the emergence of human life on Earth until today, human individual, social and ecological regimes have developed within the context of a great number of other regimes, ranging from the dominant astronomical and planetary regimes to the lesser, but mostly still dominant, organic regimes including all life-forms.

The first thing to observe when discussing the emergence of human life in relation to the history of the Universe is that the period from which remains of modern *Homo sapiens sapiens* have been recovered, which spans perhaps 100,000 to 200,000 years, is very small compared with all of history, some 10 to 20 billion years, or even the history of the Earth, 4.7 billion years according to the latest estimates. On the timescale of cosmic history, very little happened during the era in which human societies developed from small bands of gatherers and hunters to the age of space exploration. Stars and galaxies moved a little farther away from each other; a few new stars appeared in the sky, while some others exploded and subsequently vanished; unknown numbers of comets were intercepted by planets of our Solar System or burnt out; countless meteorites of different sizes impacted the Earth.

There have been some marked changes of the planetary regime as a whole in the period of modern human evolution (cf. Roberts 1989, Williams et al. 1993, van Andel 1994). A glacial period came and went, which caused great ecological changes all over the globe and set clear limits to human habitation. Also, the forces of geology continued. As a result of plate tectonics, earthquakes shook parts of the continents at more or less regular intervals. Violent movements of the sea floor, in particular, produced flood waves which, in their turn, will have posed serious risks to early coastal dwellers. Volcanoes erupted periodically, and a few volcanic islands were born along oceanic hot spot ridges.

Continental drift, another expression of plate tectonics, continually reshaped and repositioned the Earth's landmasses. This led, for instance, to a gradual expansion of the Atlantic Ocean, which is now 50 to 100 metres wider than in 1492, the year when Columbus set sail for India (cf. van Andel 1994:126). Whereas some mountain areas were uplifted observably, other regions became depressed. In only a few centuries' time or, in extreme cases, after just one earthquake, the ceaseless deformations of the Earth's crust produced effects that could easily be seen with the naked eye. The movements along the San Andreas Fault in California are well known. And in Peru, for instance, one can observe today that some Incaic irrigation canals constructed about five hundred years ago now run slightly uphill (cf. Moseley 1992:27, 262), which has led to considerable mystification about the ancient people who made them. They are said to have reigned over enigmatic lost powers to control the waters and send them up the slopes.

Yet most of the geological changes proceeded at a far slower pace than human cultural evolution.[1] The same can be said about the biological evolution of the higher species, including our own, which all need a relatively long time to reproduce. This period, c.100,000 to 200,000 years, represents about 6,000 to 12,000 human generations. The time from which agricultural societies began to dominate gatherers and hunters spans at most about 10,000 years, only some 600 generations. As a result, even the inhabitants of (post)modern societies by and large have the physiological make-up of gatherers and hunters.

In the struggle to survive and expand, human beings intentionally developed their individual, social and ecological regimes. In fact, as I suggested before, all efforts to change human regimes can be interpreted as attempts at problem solving. Most of these efforts had unintentional side effects, of course, and it may well be that the original intentions were only rarely fully realised. Nonetheless, this ever continuing process of problem solving led to a gradually increasing human influence over biological, organic and, more recently, also inorganic regimes, at least for a comparatively short period of planetary history. Armed with their growing cultural endowments, early humans began to expand over almost all the Earth, and increasingly successfully adapted to, and manipulated, the local variants of the planetary ecological regime.

Of course, not all adaptations were equally successful, and climate change could still pose a threat to established societies. "History is littered with examples of civilisations that failed to adapt [to climatic change], either because they were too set in their ways or were ruled by an elite too blinded by their own self-interest to alter the way they governed," according to US scholar Bruce Dahlin (quoted by Pain 1994:13). This would have included the Norse farmers of Greenland, Tiwanaku society in Andean Peru, early Mayan civilisation of lowland Yucatán, and the Bronze Age people of Canaan.

As a result of intensifying efforts to influence the planetary regime, especially during the last 10,000 years, humans have increasingly produced biological changes in other species. This first of all applies to the domestication of plants and animals (cf. Heiser 1990) as well as to those species which associated with the domesticates. In a number of cases, the physiological regimes of small organisms such as insects, parasites and micro-organisms including pests and diseases, which have comparatively short generations ranging from 20 minutes to days or weeks, also changed considerably during the period in which humans came to dominate the Earth. As a result, they could – and often did – adapt genetically to the effects of human cultural change (cf. McNeill 1986).

Any effective intentional social behaviour can only be achieved when some form of communication exists (cf. McNeill 1993b:vii-xiii, 1995b). Thus, the comparative evolutionary success of humans by developing their specific individual, social and ecological regimes, their cultures, is ultimately grounded in the increasing capacity to communicate with one another. This has allowed us to coordinate our ideas and behaviour on a greater scale and in more effective ways than any other species known to have lived on this planet. It may well be, as William McNeill (1995a) argues, that before early humans could speak with one another the emerging capacity of greater numbers of humans to rhythmically move together, in the form of both dance and drill, may have played an important part in coordinating their behaviour, and thus constitute larger social regimes than would have been possible otherwise. For lack of concrete evidence it will be difficult to assess the merits of this hypothesis. However, there can be little doubt that the development of symbols, expressed most notably through speech, has been vital for improving communication and social coordination, for the enlargement of human intellectual and emotional capabilities, the growing capacity for learning and, as a consequence, the development of an ever increasing variety of cultural regimes (cf. Elias 1978a, 1991, Gamble 1995). This has contributed a great deal to the growing ability of humans to survive and dominate the Earth, at least in the short term.

Although we have developed the capacity to communicate and socially coordinate our behaviour with the aid of specific behaviourial regimes further than any other species, quite a few other organisms also know forms of communication and can, therefore, be said to have social and ecological regimes of some sort. Many animals exhibit forms of learned behaviour, for instance the recognition of certain types of food. This becomes very clear when animals raised in zoos are set loose in what should be their natural habitat. Very often, they find it hard to survive, since they have not learned the ecological regime of their wild counterparts. In addition, all kinds of animal group behaviour, their 'social regimes', which have a clear survival value, are also to some extent learned. And we may suspect that the social regime developed in a zoo is often ill adapted to survival in the wild.

The same distinction can be made not only for many complex animal species but perhaps even for some plants, too. Recently, it was discovered that when attacked, some plants emit tiny amounts of gaseous molecules which may act as warning signals alerting neighbours of the same or related species and helping them to mobilize their biochemical defence mechanisms (Bruin et al. 1995). If true, such collective protective behaviour could be interpreted as a type of plant social regime. As a result of lack of academic attention, it is as yet unclear to what extent forms of plant-to-plant communication, and as a result plant social regimes, exist. It even seems that micro-organisms communicate with one another and coordinate their behaviour to some extent (Pennisi 1995), which would suggest that on this level of living microprocesses social regimes exist as well.

36

Whatever future discoveries may reveal, the increasing human capacity to communicate among ourselves and thus to coordinate our behaviour is undoubtedly the major reason for our comparative biological success. The ever growing capacity for developing social regimes with the aid of speech and symbolic reflection contributed, among other things, to new technical inventions, such as tools and fire control, as well as to their increasing efficiency. This helped the early folk to confront the challenges presented by the natural environment, including the danger of being hunted by large carnivores. In other words, social regime development stimulated improvements of the human ecological regime, at least from the hominid point of view. Slowly but surely, as the hunted became hunters, a growing power difference between hominids and other higher animals developed to the advantage of ancient humans (cf. Gamble 1995:66-70, Goudsblom 1990).

Fig. 3.1: *Artist's impression of a leopard dragging away a young hominid. At some sites, hominid bones may have accumulated as a result of such activities (from: Tattersall 1993:89)*

By acquiring increasingly refined and differentiated forms of ecological, social and individual regimes, human beings (and to some extent animals as well) not only exercised a growing influence over the surrounding natural environment but also over their own physiological regimes. Of course, human domination of their physiological regimes is limited, but some such influences can easily be observed. Today, for instance, it is impossible to know precisely to what extent aggressive and peaceful forms of behaviour are biologically or culturally determined. Emotions aroused by symbolic thought can stimulate the production of hormones that induce violent behaviour. Yet people have also learned not to act impulsively, at least not too often, according to their biological inclinations, and thus to ignore or repress their biological signals. This also applies to many other aspects of our physiological regime. As a result, it is now impossible to determine where the precise borderline between human biology and sociology may be, which has led to recurrent discussions about the importance of 'nature vs. nurture'. Regardless of where the demarcation line between biology and sociology should be drawn, however, there can be no doubt that all learned human and animal regimes have social origins.

HUMAN ECOLOGICAL REGIME TRANSFORMATIONS AS THE MAJOR STRUCTURING PRINCIPLE OF HUMAN HISTORY

Which criteria can the notion of regimes provide for structuring all of human history? Much of what follows is a summary of the position elaborated and shared by Johan Goudsblom and myself, which has been partially outlined before by Goudsblom (1989, 1992).

In a general sense, both human ecological and social regimes can be utilised as conceptual means for structuring all of human history. However, we think it is perhaps correct to say that seen from a long-term perspective, the principal changes of the human past have been marked, produced, or at least made possible, by three major human ecological regime transformations. These are: the domestication of fire; the domestication of plants and animals; and industrialization on the basis of inanimate energy, mostly fossil fuels.

It is important to see that in contrast to the development of speech, other forms of communication, and tool making, the three great ecological regime transformations are exclusively human traits. There are no other animals that have acquired these abilities. This partially justifies our choice for these developments as the major structuring principles for the human past. Of course, learning to speak and tool making have been of great importance for the development of apes into humans and also allowed the domestication of fire. Yet these developments do not provide a sufficiently clear and coherent framework for structuring all of human history.

The three major ecological regime transformations produced by humans have had far-reaching consequences for both the natural environment and the prevailing social regimes. The domestication of fire led to considerable ecological and social change, which could not have been brought about by people able to communicate and make tools but without fire control. It also provided a major precondition for the second great ecological regime transformation, the introduction of agriculture and animal husbandry. These developments, in turn, led to more ecological and social change. The same is true for industrialization. All this will be elaborated in the following section. Suffice it here to restate the well-known observation that whereas before the emergence of agriculture many, if not most, human societies were nomadic and rather egalitarian, the transition to a life based on agriculture allowed for sedentary societies with rapidly growing numbers of people, whose societies began to differentiate at an increasing speed, in particular from about 5,000 years ago. State formation and the development of the great military-agrarian empires are other conspicuous aspects of this phase. Industrialisation led, among other more obvious things such as an exploding world population, greatly expanding communication networks and unprecedented levels of production and consumption, to the spread of states to all regions on Earth, and now to an increasingly global society.

Thus, in our view, there have been three major ecological regime transformations underlying all of human history and structuring it. This is, of course, not an entirely new position. Many scholars have emphasised the importance of what we call the second and third ecological regime transformations. Usually, however, these academics have concentrated on the three dominant ecological regimes associated with these transformations, namely gatherers and hunters, agrarian and industrial societies. By contrast, the domestication of fire as the first great ecological regime transformation, which took place during the process when hominids became humans, has until now received comparatively little attention.

er to concentrate on the ecological regime transforma-
nselves rather than only on their 'outcomes', the domi-
ogical regimes, as is customary today. The transition
une ecological regime to another has usually been a long and
painful process. For an extended period, various ecological
regimes existed side by side. As a result, attention to their mutual
interactions is of supreme importance in order to understand the
dynamics of human history. Thus, we focus not solely on, for
example, agrarian societies, but rather on what we call the "agrarianisation process". The prevalence of agrarian societies as the
dominant mode of production was the outcome of a long process,
as well as the precondition for the next ecological regime transformation, industrialisation.

What happens in general terms when differentials of ecological skills develop? As William McNeill has often emphasised
and elaborated, most notably in his opus magnum *The Rise of the
West*: when a society acquires superior skills, those in contact with
it are presented with a problem. Various types of reactions are
possible: the outsiders can attempt to acquire these skills also, or
they can try to resist or ignore them. Both types of reactions
occur. In the first case, the innovation spreads and becomes dominant, while power differentials that develop during the process
are smoothed out in the course of time. In the second case, the
societies resisting or ignoring the new skills may lag behind and
become less powerful, although in the long run this is certainly
not always the inevitable result. Resisting change can have a direct
unsuspected pay-off, or may confer unplanned advantages some-
time in the future. Seen from a long-term perspective, the technical innovations associated with the first two major ecological
regime transformations, the domestication of fire and agrarianisation, have become dominant, and thus have spread all over the
world, while we are currently witnessing the spread of industrialisation around the globe.

According to Goudsblom (1989:19), there is one single very
simple and illuminating model, consisting of three stages, that
underlies all these processes. It can be summarised as follows. In
all cases there was a stage in which no one had 'it', for instance
control over fire. Then, a stage came in which some people had
'it', while others did not. The last stage was reached when all people had acquired 'it'. And, I may add, in many cases a fourth stage

40

came, when some people could afford to abandon 'it' because they had acquired new and better means, while others still needed 'it'. The last stage is reached when no one has 'it' any longer. This model is not only applicable to ecological regime transformations; it is in operation with all innovations, social as well as technical.

In many cases, the first three stages are sufficient to describe human history. When we apply the model to more specific examples such as, for instance, the introduction of the steam engine, it becomes clear that the fourth stage has been reached (when we restrict ourselves to the design of James Watt; today, various types of steam turbines are omnipresent, of course). Nowadays, in most North Atlantic societies steam engines can only been found in museums, while in other parts of the world, most notably India and China, steam power is still driving trains and factories. The steam engine is not the only such example. Also the first great ecological regime, the life based on gathering and hunting, has reached the fourth stage, while its first and second stages never existed. There was simply never a period in early human history in which self-supporting social groups survived without collecting or hunting food.[2] Industrialisation, by contrast, is now passing through its second stage.

Another attraction of concentrating on ecological regime transformations as the major structuring principle of human history is that this neatly fits into the way of structuring big history presented here, which can only be achieved by looking at ecological regimes, since most of macrohistory has been inanimate. Is this just a happy coincidence, I wonder? Would this theoretical choice perhaps reflect the (post)modern unease about what humans are doing to 'the environment'? Or does this insight indeed point to the often underestimated importance, at least in the humanities, of the biological and physical aspects of human life, even in culture? I would think that the last suggestion is the most relevant one, but the importance of the recent greater attention to matters environmental in ordinary life and its consequences in academic thought should not be lost sight of. It would be very optimistic and thoroughly unsociological to assume that in contrast to what our predecessors have achieved, our thinking would develop completely dissociated from current societal developments.

41

In order to avoid possible misunderstandings, I want to emphasise the following. In our view, the "human adventure on Earth" is not predetermined and has no meanings others than those attributed to it by the people themselves. As both Norbert Elias and William McNeill have often emphasised, the direction of human history is unplanned and blind, although it is the outcome of a great many planned and intentional acts and decisions (including those of not to act) of all the people who have ever lived on this planet.

Neither do we think that all societies pass through all stages of a predetermined evolutionary path. On the contrary, the focus on Goudsblom's simple model mentioned above helps to remind us that, for instance, some societies began to industrialise when others were still in the pre-agrarian stage. Contacts between them led to new developments, which can to some extent be compared with those between agrarian and gatherer-hunter societies, but which had some novel features as well.

Societies may also regress. For example, according to US anthropologist Anna Roosevelt, this may have happened in the Amazon region, when agrarian societies began to succumb to European diseases on a massive scale. Some of the survivors would have returned to a life based on gathering and hunting (quoted by Pain 1993:8). In other words, for every trend, a counter-trend may be observed. When contemplating human history, we first of all need to establish which trends were the dominant ones in a given period. Thus, while perhaps for local reasons some societies may have regressed, there can be no doubt that the major trends in human history have been towards agrarianisation and later industrialisation and not the reverse.

Like all aspects of big history, human history is "underdetermined", to borrow a phrase from the US biologist Stephen Jay Gould (1994:63). Our general models provide generalised structures of and explanations for our past, but cannot explain precisely why, when and how everything happened as it did. For instance, although historians have convincingly outlined many aspects of the early stages of the industrialisation process, we are unable to fully explain why and how the industrial mode began to develop first in Britain when it did so, and not anywhere else on this planet. We can safely say, however, that without the preceding transition to an agricultural way of life, industrialisation would not have been possible. Also, the evolution of the Universe, Solar System, Earth, life, and even microprocesses cannot be fully explained by our prevailing grand models and, as a consequence, are all underdetermined (cf. Cushing 1994:199-202).

In this respect, the social and natural sciences have more in common than most people would perhaps suspect. Sociology and meteorology, for example, both deal with complex unstable configurations that are unique in character, in which situations never repeat themselves exactly, and in which small causes can have large effects. As I said before, these features of non-linear processes are very common in nature, as modern chaos theoreticians increasingly realise (cf. Gleick 1988). As a result of the characteristics of both atmospheric and social configurations, the predictive power of the process models is limited. Nonetheless, in retrospect one can continually observe patterns and regularities, which implies that the developments are not completely random.

The focus on regime transformations, including all the varieties and power differentials that develop during such processes, affords a more dynamic and reality-congruent view of history than the picture which results from concentrating largely or exclusively on the dominant type of society which developed in a certain period as a result of these transformations. In other words, looking at transition processes and the developing phase differentials instead of only focusing on their 'outcomes' not only helps us to attain a better image of the past but also provides more refined and simple explanations for what happened in history. This applies not only to ecological regime transformations but also to important social regime transformations, such as the emergence of states.

All three major human ecological regimes have had pervasive implications for the prevailing social regimes. For instance, depending on the region, gathering and hunting – with or without fire – necessitated certain lifestyles or, in other words, a specific type of social regime. The same applies to agrarian and industrial regimes.

All great ecological regime transformations were ongoing processes. As Goudsblom has argued in *Fire and Civilization* (1992), the domestication of fire never reached a point where inventions were no longer made. The same applies to the a-grarianisation process and industrialisation. When the transition to an agrarian lifestyle began, the process of fire domestication had reached its third stage ('all have it') already a long time ago. By contrast, at the onset of the industrial revolution, the agrarianisation process was only in its second stage ('some have it, others not'). It is only recently that worldwide social contrasts may be diminishing. Of course, there are still enormous differences both within the industrialised countries and between them and less-industrialised regions. Although very difficult to determine with any degree of precision, it appears to me that these differences are perhaps less pronounced than they were a century ago.

Three major ecological regime transformations as structuring principle for human history

THE FIRST GREAT ECOLOGICAL REGIME TRANSFORMA-TION: THE DOMESTICATION OF FIRE

The first major ecological regime transformation was the domestication of fire. The importance of this process has been explored by Johan Goudsblom (1992), and what follows here is mostly a summary of his analysis. All modern humans, whose remains emerge in the fossil record from about 100,000 BP depending on the region, appear to have known the use of fire. The period in which fire started to be used may stretch much further back in time, perhaps to about 1.5 million years ago. More concrete evidence for fire control dates back to 500,000 years ago, still a long time before modern humans appeared on the planetary stage.

For lack of sufficient archaeological evidence it is impossible to describe in any detail what the consequences of fire control have been. However, it seems reasonable to suspect that Goudsblom's simple 'phase model' mentioned above – first no one has 'it', then some, and then all – also applies to the domestication of fire. In the period of early hominid exploits, there was a number of different subspecies. Now, there is only one humankind. How did this come about, and what happened to those subspecies that went extinct? Would the differential domestication of fire have played any role in this development? Goudsblom has suggested that the possession of fire control may have been of decisive importance in an elimination contest that would have taken place both within and among the various hominid subgroups, as a result of which only the fire-possessing victors survived. An alternative, more peaceful scenario suggests a gradual spread of this skill over the various subspecies. This does not, however, shed any light on the currently unsolved question of why only one human species evolved, able to control fire, and why the rest disappeared.

At the time when modern humans appeared, 100,000 to 200,000 years ago, most if not all the existing hominids, including the Neanderthal people, had achieved some degree of fire control. The possession of fire, or the lack of it, can, therefore, not fully explain the final elimination contest. However, power differences did not only develop between people with or without fire control, but also between those who possessed fire skills to a greater or lesser extent. Modern *Homo sapiens* may well have been able to control fire more effectively, and thus would have had greater survival chances than those with less elaborate fire skills. Of course, this is all speculation, and hard evidence for these hypotheses will be difficult to find.

Whatever the merits of these ideas, the development of a human fire regime had further consequences, both ecological and social, which can be seen as a growing human influence on the regimes of plants and larger animals (cf. Goudsblom 1990) and, as a result, also on the insects and microparasites that fed on these species. First, some examples of such ecological effects. Humans could intentionally burn the landscape in order to favour certain plant species and diminish others. In addition, predators could be kept at greater distances, while fire control also facilitated the hunting of big game or the clearing of woods to provide pasture for game animals. Burning the earth may have gone on for millennia, if not much longer, and is still happening in many areas in tropical Africa, Asia and the Americas. Thus, through fire control humans may have changed the face of the Earth for much longer than is often thought, and may have influenced the biological and inanimate planetary regimes for an unknown period and to an unfathomable extent.

Fig. 4.1: *Artist's impression of a Homo erectus band living in a fire-lit cave,*
keeping predators at a distance (from: Gould 1993:243)

It is very hard to assess such possible effects. Although the numbers of early humans were very low, their burning operations
could still have had far-reaching consequences, especially since we
may assume that now and then the fires went out of control and
burnt stretches larger than planned. It may well be that as a result
of human burning, a fire-accustomed vegetation developed in
many places, the tropics and subtropics in particular, including
the proliferation of fire-loving species whose seeds only sprout
after a good burn (cf. Goudsblom 1992:14-15, Goudie 1987:26
ff.). In the words of US writer Larry O'Hanlon:

> When humans tamed fire more than 500 000 years ago, they
> acquired an effective way of cleaning out the old debris to stimu-
> late new, vigorous plant growth, and hence improve hunting and
> foraging. People quickly took over from lightning strikes as the
> leading starters of fires. In a classic example of ecological feedback,
> the flora and fauna of these fire-dependent ecologies in Australia,

South Africa and California adapted to human-managed fire regimes, in which fires were probably more frequent and less intense than they had been before. The result can be seen today in innumerable fire-adapted species. The heat of a quick ground fire is known to trigger some pine cones to open and release their seeds. Other seeds have wax-like coatings that have to be melted off before germination. [...] If fire is excluded, such species struggle to survive (1995:32).[1]

Of course this represents only indirect evidence. It may be difficult to find clear signs of early human action as a root cause of the emergence of fire-loving species. Burning the land would have left few traces. But perhaps some of these traces still exist, and we only need to direct our attention correctly. More likely than not, as Peter Westbroek suggested, they might be discovered in off-shore marine sediments rather than on land, since in the tropics, where most of the burning would have taken place, only a few sites have been formed with thick sediment sequences stretching back a sufficient period of time.

Whatever the effects on the landscape and on shifts in balances between biological regimes, other consequences of fire control were profound. It led to a considerable enlargement of the human ecological niche and, as a result, to a growing dominance over other animals as well as to increasing human numbers. Through cooking, roasting and other comparable types of food preparation with the aid of fire, the range of edible foodstuffs was expanded enormously, and thus, in general, human exploitation of nature. Burning fires allowed people to live in colder climates and, consequently, contributed to the first spread of early humans out of Africa over large parts of the Earth (cf. Gamble 1995, Goudie 1987:26-34, Simmons 1994:38-42, Williams et al. 1993:190-221). This also implied that they could escape the ever-raging tropical diseases which, in turn, may have contributed to population growth (McNeill 1985:35-39).

Just as, much later, the agrarian regime would prove to be a major precondition for the industrialisation of society, likewise the fire regime was a necessary precondition for agrarianisation. It is hard to imagine that any sedentary agrarian life would have been possible for long without control over fire of various kinds. For instance, most agrarian foodstuffs need a heat treatment of some sort before they are edible. In addition, the use of fire, and of smoke in particular, helped to preserve food, most notably meat and fish. More importantly, perhaps, most of the land to be cultivated could only have been cleared efficiently for agrarian use by burning.

THE GATHERER-HUNTER SOCIAL REGIME

The domestication of fire had considerable effects on the social and individual regimes of gatherer-hunter societies. Greater control over fire could only have been achieved by increasing self-control. During the many millennia in which early humans gradually mastered the use of fire, humans also learnt and internalised growing and differentiating forms of self-restraint. This, in turn, could only have come about through the exercise of external pressure of some sort, if only expressed in educating the younger generations about the possibilities and dangers the control of fire presented. As a result, the effort to reign over the forces of fire may have stimulated the need for more intense social interaction, and thus contributed to a growing ability to communicate and think in abstract terms.

Here we may suspect some effects of the evolving cultural regime on the human physiological regime. The period between the incipient domestication of fire and early agrarianisation, about 30,000 generations, is long enough to allow for some genetic selection of human aptitude in these matters. As a result, the efforts to control fire may have contributed considerably in establishing the remarkable mouldability of the human character, the ability to learn and transmit behaviour to a much greater extent than any other species, in other words culture. In addition to developing forms of communication and coordination such as speaking, dancing, music making (cf. Buckley 1994) and perhaps art production, the cultural effects of fire control may have been among the driving forces behind the development of the potentiality of culture as a genetically determined species-specific trait.

For a long time, the fire domesticators lived as gatherers and hunters, on a diet that varied from place to place according to the circumstances. The world population slowly grew, and more and more parts of the Earth became inhabited. As a result, local and regional population pressure remained rather low. Judging from surviving artifacts, mostly flint tools, which are remarkably similar all over the world during the greater part of at least the last 500,000 years, technical skills appear to have developed slowly. The same seems to apply to social organisation. For a long time, humanity formed one single, very loosely connected network which shared many characteristics and exhibited only limited local variations. In comparison with later periods, communication in the form of messages and material exchanges went slowly, while local cultural developments did likewise. Consequently, inventions could easily spread everywhere before any group developed a decisive cultural advantage.

The life of the early gatherers and hunters was very much determined by the opportunities and limitations offered by the surrounding natural environment, by human nature, as well as by technical skills, social knowledge, and forms of organisation – presumably basically through kinship – such people had attained. During this early, by far the longest, phase of human development, all people were involved in the ecological regime. They were obliged to follow the seasonal patterns, to go where the food was, while they had to avoid over-exploiting the natural resources in order to avoid undermining their own subsistence base.

Especially during early human history, before modern *Homo sapiens* appeared, a period stretching from perhaps 500,000 to about 100,000 BP, only very limited social differentiation seems to have taken place, both within and between bands. This apparent stability of the gatherer-hunter social regime was connected to both the paramount importance of the human ecological regime prevailing and the more limited cultural skills the early humans possessed. While the human ecological regime never fully determines the social regime, a particular ecological regime places certain constraints on it. Clearly, the need to make a living by gathering and hunting, with fire or without, determined social life to a considerable extent. Since most gatherer and hunter bands were obliged to follow the food, and because food resources were not abundant all year round in many, if not most places, early humans simply had to live a nomadic life.

This way of living may also have had a decisive influence on the ways the early folk solved their internal conflicts. As long as there were enough land and resources available, a subgroup could

50

always split off when part of the band tried to impose itself. This would have prevented any extensive form of social differentiation and the formation of a stable hierarchy beyond the kinship stage. Thus, while in egalitarian bands and tribal societies inequality was perhaps always struggling to get out, the nomadic lifestyle in a situation of comparatively low population pressure made it impossible for any members of the band to gain the upper hand for themselves and their offspring (Mann 1987:42 ff., Sanderson 1995:175). It was only when people entered the stage of sedentary life that such developments could emerge.

It appears impossible to know to what extent early gatherer-hunter societies engaged in violent encounters. Most modern anthropological studies as well as many West European explorers' reports about gatherers and hunters suggest that in cases of confrontation they tended to flee rather than fight. This may, however, be a pattern such people developed out of long experience with more powerful neighbours who had turned to agriculture and had become more powerful as a result. I doubt if we can establish how gatherers and hunters treated, and reacted to, their neighbours before the arrival of agriculture and animal husbandry. Modern palaeo-anthropological research suggests that early human development was made possible because of the need of hominids on the growing African savannas to defend themselves against predators. As defensive and offensive tools became more efficient, they also began to hunt a greater variety of animals. This may well have led to some violence among their own kind as well, in particular when resources of various kinds were perceived as becoming scarce. For example, from an examination of ancient rock paintings, the Australian anthropologists Paul Taçon and Christopher Chippindale concluded that this was the case among Australian Aborigines at least from around 6,000 BP to the turn of this century (1994:211-248). The timing would again be related to "the final rise in world sea levels about 6000 years ago" which changed local conditions (1994:217). In the subsequent discussion, Canadian anthropologist Joan Vastokas mentioned a considerable number of similar cases in other regions of the world (Taçon & Chippindale 1994:238-240). I suspect that the nomadic people would have tended to steer away from conflicts with their neighbours as long as there was enough free land available. When population pressure rose and/or people settled down more or less permanently, the tendency to defend themselves would have increased.

When modern humans began spreading across the Earth, they left artifacts testifying to increasingly refined technology and social organisation. Most notably, the period from 40,000 BP until the time when the agrarian revolution began to take off was characterised by a growing cultural expertise in dealing both with the natural environment and with other people. Increasing social differentiation, presumably largely within kinship networks (which may have been very elaborate) but also among groups through economic and symbolic exchanges, was characteristic of gatherers and hunters in many areas around the globe. These developments may have been connected with a growing scarcity of free land and resources. Some division of labour took place, such as flint mining, other forms of work, and perhaps trade. It may well be that in the course of time, people were forced to search for new means of living as they depleted their known resources. Archaeological evidence from many parts of the world suggests that when large animals became extinct, presumably partially as a result of hunting but also through climate change, humans increasingly depended on chasing smaller game, on gathering plants and on exploiting aquatic resources (Cohen 1977).

SEDENTARY GATHERERS AND HUNTERS

The planetary climate regime, which fluctuates more or less regularly when seen from a long-term perspective, strongly influenced the opportunities for gatherers and hunters to make a living. Ice ages came and went, which meant that people had to adapt to drastically changing climatological circumstances. This included migration southwards in large parts of the Eurasian continent and back, as well as downward and upward movements in mountainous areas. As another consequence of these climatological changes, varying sea levels placed shifting limits on the size and shape of coastal areas suitable for human habitation. It is only rarely recognised in the social sciences that from about 5,000 BP until today, the sea level has been higher than during the last c.100,000 years, during which modern humans appear to have emerged (Roberts 1989, Williams et al. 1993, van Andel 1994:77-

87). In the past 5,000 years, human populations have tended to concentrate near or along coastlines, in particular close to river estuaries or along river banks. I think that a careful consideration of this observation in connection with the lower sea levels prevailing during the rest of the last glacial period, which witnessed the emergence of modern humans, may significantly alter our view on early human history.

In order to explain this in more detail, let us first look at some examples of more recent coastal-dwelling hunter and gatherer communities. The perhaps best-known case is presented by Amerindians living along the Northwestern Pacific coast. They were fishing societies which could be (and needed to be) sedentary because of the specific nature and abundance of the marine resources they depended on, most notably salmon and candlefish. This was thanks to regional effects of the planetary regime that stimulated a cold sea current which, in turn, favoured the growth of many marine species. These natural resources may have been very rich, but they were not present all year round. As a response, a type of storage regime developed to survive the lean seasons. Consequently, these people had to live a sedentary life since they had become bound to their supplies and, therefore, also to one another. In terms of British sociologist Michael Mann, such societies had become 'caged' (1987:39 ff.). As in all sedentary societies, inequality could now succeed in struggling out.

It is therefore not surprising that in many such fishing communities along the Canadian Pacific coast, considerable social differentiation, including the emergence of a redistributive leadership, had already taken place by the time explorers of West-European extraction began to descend on them in the eighteenth century (cf. Drucker 1963, Efrat & Langlois 1978, Weinberg 1978). The scarce archaeological evidence suggests that this indigenous social structure had already existed hundreds of years before the arrival of modern Europeans.

There is considerable evidence of similar developments in other areas where hunting and gathering could sustain a sedentary life. US archaeologist Mark Cohen described many examples of early coastal sedentary societies on various continents mainly subsisting on aquatic resources (1977). This suggests that such developments would take place sooner or later when the regional non-human ecological regimes were favourable. For example, the ecological situation along the Northwest coast of what is now Canada is mirrored along the Southern Pacific coast of South America. French archaeologist Claude Chauchat gave the following description of the interplay between geological, climatological and biological aspects of the planetary regime that produced this situation in the southern hemisphere. In Chauchat's words:

> The ultimate factors affecting the climate on the Peruvian coast result from the rotation of the planet. The Coriolis force tends to deviate any moving fluid at a right angle from its original direction. This and other factors create a pattern of air and water circulation which determines the existence of permanent, stationary high-pressure zones near the centres of the oceans in both hemispheres. [...] Centrifugal winds radiate from this zone, pushing water along. This surface water is in turn forced to the west and, near the Peruvian coast, tends to move away from the shore, where it is replaced by a deep, cold-water current. [...] Nutrients are prevented from falling slowly to the ocean floor and are forced to remain in the immediately subsurface waters where photosynthesis is at its maximum. From phytoplankton to birds and sea mammals, the whole marine ecosystem is thus multiplied and the Peruvian coast swarms with life. It is natural, then, that almost from the beginning marine resources have been important to the inhabitants of the Peruvian coast (1988:42-43).

As a result, at least from around 5,000 BP, sedentary societies exhibiting considerable social differentiation developed all along the Southern Pacific coast mainly based on the exploitation of marine resources (cf. Arriaza 1995, Bray et al. 1989, Bruhns 1994, Fiedel 1992, Fung P. 1988, Moseley 1992). In Europe and Asia, similar patterns have been observed (Mithen in: Cunliffe 1994: 119-127, Cohen 1977, Roberts 1989). It is likely that further research, including a systematic literature review, will reveal such patterns along most, if not all, coastal areas where the abundance of natural resources allowed these developments to take place, as long as there were no major ecological impediments, of course, such as ice-covered land all year round.

However, what happened before the oceans reached their all-time high level at around 5,000 BP? I imagine that also before that time sedentary societies based on fishing, hunting and gathering would have existed along the shores of the seven seas, the traces of which may be waiting for underwater archaeological exploration to be revealed. In other words, in order to produce a more complete picture of early human development, a promising approach would be to 'excavate' offshore, in principle everywhere in the world where human habitation has been possible. In all likelihood, such remains will be covered by deep layers of alluvial and marine sediments, which will not facilitate the digging, but which may have contributed to preserving whatever traces of early human life may still linger in such places. Thus, I would suggest that during most of the history of modern humankind, a substantial proportion of early hunters and gatherers may well have been sedentary fishers who perhaps knew considerable social differentiation, and that the dominant view of almost exclusively nomadic, rather egalitarian, hunters and gatherers may be in need of some revision.[2]

To summarise: although the importance of sedentary gatherer-hunter societies may have been underestimated, generally speaking, the gatherer-hunter regime never showed anything approaching the elaborated social hierarchy that would become the hallmark of agrarian-based state societies. This did not happen because it could not happen, in part because of the tendency to split off in case of conflicts, a feasible option as long as there was enough free land available, and also because in many cases the ecological regime could not support such a sedentary hierarchy for long. The gathering-hunting regime simply placed more constraints on the social regime than any ecological regime that followed.

THE SECOND GREAT ECOLOGICAL REGIME TRANSFORMATION: THE TRANSITION TO AN AGRARIAN REGIME

When agriculture and animal husbandry began to be practised, a new ecological regime came into being, while the older one was gradually marginalised, or even disappeared. The currently accepted view is that the transition to agriculture proceeded slowly, and that it will be very difficult to say precisely when these developments began. This is partially caused by the problem of how to define domestication. Some scientists speak of domestication only when the species brought under human control altered genetically as a result. However, I think that defining domestication in this way obscures the social developments that led to such human-induced genetic changes. In my view, the best definition of domestication is: human efforts to actively influence the reproductive chances of other species.

By looking at domestication in this way, its incipient stage appears to have begun a great deal earlier than is usually assumed. For instance, by burning the landscape at set times, hunters and gatherers may have attempted to encourage the expansion of grasslands. This would have favoured the growth of plant and animal species gathered or hunted by humans such as wild cereals and game animals, which were later domesticated (Lewis 1972, Cohen 1977:21-27, Fiedel 1992:168, Harris 1990, Reed 1976, Smith 1995:16-18). In this and other ways, hunters and gatherers may have influenced the ecological balances to an extent and for a period of time yet unknown. Thus, the incipient transition to agriculture and animal husbandry may well have been a very prolonged and gradual process which could have taken place all over the globe.

Traces of these efforts as well as of other early attempts at domestication may be very difficult to find, if they have been preserved at all. Recently, however, some interesting claims have been made which, if true, may radically alter our view of the beginning of agrarianisation. In 1992, Leigh Dayton reported that the Australian scientists Matthew Spriggs, Stephen Wickler and Thomas Loy had discovered in the Solomon Islands traces of domesticated taro strains on ancient tools dating back some 28,000 years. The British archaeologist Gordon Hillman would have found "grinding stones and tubers at Wadi Kubbaniya, a site in Egypt, which is between 17 000 and 18 000 years old" (Dayton 1992:14). Thus, I think that the current view, based on the solid factual evidence of emerging domesticated species, which states that these developments began about 10,000 years ago, is in all likelihood too restricted.

Until today, the reasons behind this large ecological regime transformation are not fully understood, and this is not the place to outline the academic discussion in any great detail (cf. Budiansky 1992, Cohen 1977, Fiedel 1992, Heiser 1990, Redman 1978, Simmons 1994, Sanderson 1995, Smith 1995). Judging from the literature quoted by these authors, none of the books I consulted provides a reasonably complete overview. However, some general features of the second great ecological regime transformation have emerged.

First of all, a clear acceleration of these developments, usually called the neolithic revolution, took place almost simultaneously, seen from a long-term perspective, between c.10,000 and 8,000 BP, in several tropical and sub-tropical areas all over the globe. Clear evidence for the rapid emergence of an agricultural regime based on domesticated species has been found in regions as far apart as the Fertile Crescent, South-East Asia and Andean Peru.[3] This means that from that time, the transition to the agrarian way of life clearly began to gather speed. People not only stepped up their efforts to improve the reproductive chances of the species they found attractive but also began to exert growing selective pressures within certain species. This led to genetic alterations in the favoured plants and animals and thus to the emergence of domesticated species, which had greater reproductive chances than their untamed counterparts as long as humans were willing to take care of them. In the process, humans and a comparatively small set of food plants and animals became increasingly dependent on each other.

The concurrent timing of all these developments on a planetary scale may be accidental. But if not, it would suggest that a global cause with similar effects was involved which may have initiated these developments, or at least strengthened an already existing trend. Alternatively, all these areas may have been so well-interconnected that the idea of domestication could spread rapidly all over the world and was applied when and where it was deemed necessary. Although in the course of time diffusion of agrarian techniques obviously took place from the early centres of domestication, it is currently considered unlikely that all these early centres were sufficiently interlinked as early as 10,000 BP to allow this (cf. Fiedel 1992:349-366).

The prime candidate for a global factor involved in triggering the emergence of the agricultural regime is climate change. The last glacial period had ended about two millennia earlier, around 12,000 BP. This was a rather abrupt change. For a similar steep rise in temperature we need to go back to about 125,000 years ago, when modern humans were not yet around in most places (cf. Gamble in: Cunliffe 1994:18, Wright Jr. in: Reed 1976:281-318). Thus, both this formidable global change of the climatological regime, in its turn the result of regular changes in the earthly astronomical regime, and the worldwide change toward an agricultural regime were produced almost simultaneously for the first time in modern human history, which suggests more than mere coincidence.

However, the mechanism by which the warming up of the climate would have favoured the domestication of plants and animals has not been sufficiently elucidated. There can be little doubt that it stimulated the spread of certain plants and animals that were subsequently domesticated. But it is unclear to what extent climatic change would have led to unfavourable circumstances for other species on which gatherers and hunters depended in or near the regions where domestication first took off.

The transition to agriculture and animal husbandry in various parts of the world did not follow the same pattern everywhere. In some areas, people began to cultivate edible seeds first, while in other places, gourds, cotton and peppers became the earliest agrarian products, which does not point to any great need for domesticated food. Shifting cultivation developed in tropical mountainous regions such as highland Papua New Guinea from about 9,000 BP, seemingly independently of the emergence of sedentary agriculture in the Middle East (Renfrew & Bahn 1991:228-229).

Just as no single society can be said to have provided the archetype of fire control or of industrialisation, so no region should be seen as offering the standard model for agrarianisation either. Yet some common characteristics of this process can be discerned (cf. Smith 1995). All the early centres of plant domestication appear to have been subtropical or tropical mountainous areas with a considerable variation of microclimates. They were rich in local resources but probably circumscribed by more harsh surroundings. The first domesticates were often wild plants that were subsequently introduced in microclimates where they did not occur naturally.[4] US archaeologist Bruce Smith summarised his position as follows:

Climatic pressures and population growth appear to have contributed to the process, at a distance, by producing resource gradients and hardening cultural boundaries around rich resources. It wouldn't have been easy to simply move to a better location when times were hard; these societies would have needed a way of dealing with the possibilities of hard times right where they were. Within these zones, too, population growth or other factors might have heightened the ever-present fear of resource shortfall, even in times of abundance, pushing societies to increase the yield and reliability of some food resources, and pointing the way to domestication (1995:211).

British archaeologist David Harris (1990) has emphasised that in order to understand the long and slow transition to agriculture, we need to look at the seasonal variation of the food supply. While some periods of the year may have provided abundant food to gatherers and hunters, the leaner seasons would have implied food scarcity. When growing population pressure and declining natural resources as a result of over-exploitation and/or climatic change aggravated this situation, efforts to counter these problems may have led to the development of a regime of food storage in the form of seeds, nuts and herds, which then would slowly have developed into agricultural and pastoral regimes.

People would first have settled near rich food resources. Growing population pressure and perhaps deteriorating climatic conditions would have pressured the early farmers and herders to devote ever more attention to the well-being of the plants and beasts they had come to depend on. As a result, they slowly but surely converted to agrarian ways of life. This would partially explain why the transition took place gradually, as well as why agrarianising societies continued to combine agriculture with gathering and hunting for a long time.

Although the domestication of untamed species began to take off at least 10,000 years ago, the incorporation of wild species into the human fold as well as the further refinement of tamed flora and fauna is an ever-ongoing process. The modern fishing industry provides a case in point. It is still a continuation of ancient hunter and gatherer practices. Today, we witness the rapid over-exploitation of marine resources as a result of intensive fishing as well as, for example, the rise of salmon 'farms' along the Norwegian coast. In other words, the domestication of fish is gathering speed only now, although it began a long time ago (cf. Spier 1992). In the course of time, the agrarian regime intensified and diversified into, for example, dry land farming, irrigation cultivation, horticulture, etc. and various types of animal keeping.

Not only were new species regularly introduced, but also novel skills were continuously added to the technical repertoire. In particular the invention of the animal-drawn plough, the coupling of animal power to plant production, perhaps as long ago as 6500 BP made agriculture a great deal more efficient. This development can be regarded as the secondary agricultural revolution.[5] It could, of course, only happen in areas where suitable animals were available. In the Americas, such beasts were absent and, as a result, the secondary agricultural revolution only took off when Spaniards introduced the traction plough together with the needed animals of Eurasian descent, usually oxen. Also, the ever

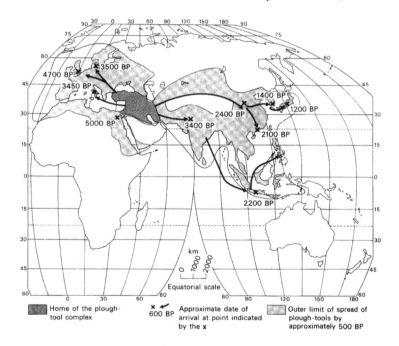

Fig. 4.2: *The spread of plough agriculture in the Old World (from: Goudie 1987:19)*

continuing intentional spread of cultivates all over the world formed part of these developments (cf. Crosby 1972, 1993). This was usually followed by the often unplanned expansion of their predators.

Domestication was not only favourable for humans but also for the happy few beasts and plants that came under human custody. While descendants of many of these species thrive in greater numbers than ever before, most undomesticated larger animals and plants fared less well. During the last ten millennia, their numbers regularly declined through hunting and gathering, or simply through habitat reduction or destruction. Today, many such species survive in small numbers only because humans protect them against other humans, either in natural reserves or in zoos. Like the fate of wild species, also the fortune of their domesticated counterparts is strongly determined by human interests. Whenever humans stopped caring for them, their numbers rapidly dwindled. In other words, tamed plants and beasts had become a great deal more dependent on humans than the other way around.

The shifting ecological balances through human action has had some unplanned consequences. Habitat destruction for some species implied habitat creation or extension for others. For instance, grain cultivation will have attracted growing numbers of mice which, in turn, may have attracted birds that preyed on them. The need to protect the harvest against such predators led, among other things, to the introduction of cats into the agrarian regime.

The intensification of the agrarian regime meant that certain plant and animal species became ever more concentrated in growing numbers. This created favourable circumstances for the micro-organisms that fed on them. As a result, plant and animal diseases became more frequent, which led to human efforts to counter them.[6] Because of the considerable genetic and physiological differences between human beings and the domesticated flora, plant pests cannot make the jump to humans. However, many animal diseases can, and have done so in the course of time (cf. McNeill 1985). As a result, the growing intimacy between humans and beasts implied increasing risks of disease transfer, and necessitated efforts to cure humans from the new illnesses.

It appears likely that women cultivated the first plants, while men domesticated animals. Although firm evidence is lacking, this would have been a logical extension of the traditional gender roles in gatherer-hunter societies, in which women used to gather and men hunted. When the traction plough was introduced, men began to take on the task of ploughing which, until then, would have been a largely female prerogative. This, in turn, would imply that women were gradually pushed back to the developing domestic sphere. As a result, this period may have witnessed the emergence of the male-dominated public domain.

The introduction of the agrarian regime led to a growing social differentiation between the early agriculturists and gatherer-hunter societies. Goudsblom's simple phase model is very suitable to characterise this transformation in general terms. Sedentary farmers and nomadic pastoralists developed in the midst of gatherer-hunter bands. The possessors of the new skills became more powerful and expanded. The neighbours either acquired these new skills, too, or were gradually pushed to marginal areas where the new regimes were less effective in earning a living than the older skills. In some, if not many cases, such marginalised societies became extinct. Many Amerindian societies, but also the Tasmanians, offer sad examples of these developments. As a result, agricultural and pastoral regimes spread to wherever the circumstances allowed. Adaptations to different ecological conditions led to a growing variation of agricultural and pastoral ways of life. This process has perhaps reached its third phase – all have 'it' – only very recently.

THE EVOLVING AGRARIAN SOCIAL REGIME

The emergence of the agrarian regime led to a profound transformation of the social regime. While in the terminology of US anthropologist Eric Wolf (1982:88 ff.) production remained kinordered, many other aspects of the social regime changed almost beyond recognition.

First of all, since the early plant cultivators became tied to the land they had come to depend on, they also became more tightly bound to one another. In the words of Michael Mann, early sedentary villages became 'social cages', in which people lived in larger numbers and greater concentrations than ever before. Judging by the growing expertise with which all kinds of things, such as houses, pottery, agricultural implements and jewellery, were made, the division of labour clearly gathered speed. The emerging pastoral nomads, by contrast, had to keep moving, which did not allow for such developments, at least not to a similar degree.

Within agrarianising societies, processes of social differentiation accelerated, which indicates that the agrarian regime allowed for it in a much greater way than the hunter-gatherer regime had done before. Depending on the opportunities and potentialities the natural ecological regime of the region offered, people became either predominantly sedentary agriculturists (including swidden cultivators) or nomadic pastoralists living on extended grasslands, steppes and savannas. While the sedentary folk could – and did – acquire and maintain material possessions to an extent greater than ever before, they became more vulnerable to attack, too, since they became tied to their land and possessions (cf. Mann 1987). Nomadic pastoralists, by contrast, were dependent on a food supply that could move also. Especially after horses were tamed for military use, nomads could attack, rob and flee almost with impunity. As a result, tense relations of various kinds between sedentary agriculturists and nomadic pastoralists developed all over the globe.

In mountainous areas such as the Andes, by contrast, nomadic pastoralists had fewer opportunities for fleeing, since that meant climbing increasingly inhospitable mountains instead of running away on seemingly endless savannas. While the Altiplano highlands will have offered some chances for successful flight, ascending a high mountain top laden with booty chased by angry villagers is not an attractive prospect. Seen from the Andean herders' point of view, the lack of any animals that could be mounted aggravated the situation, at least on the Altiplano. In most other, usually very rugged, Andean regions, this would hardly have made any difference. It is therefore not surprising that in the Andean mountains, the relations between the valley folk and the herders were much more cooperative than on the Eurasian plains, although still tense (cf. Murra 1975). I suspect that this represents a general pattern of relations among mountain dwellers (cf. Guillet 1983).

The emerging agrarian social regime, in its turn, may well have stimulated an intensification of the prevailing ecological regime. Bruce Smith explained this very succinctly:

> A newly sedentary people living in larger settlements would need new forms of social integration and interaction and new rules for the ownership and control of land and its resources. These changes may have encouraged the production of a greater harvest surplus, if such a surplus could have been used to establish and maintain contracts in a variety of ways: they could have been lent out to relatives or neighbors in times of need, offered up for community celebrations, or paid out as a dowry or brideprice when a marriage formed a new alliance between families. There are, then, a variety of social forces, other than competitive feasting, that could have encouraged family groups to invest more of their time manipulating seed plants in an effort to increase harvest yields and storable surplus (1995:211-212).

Thus, a continuous interaction between the agrarian ecological and social regimes produced the dynamics characteristic of these early societies. The stage had been set for a type of peasant life which would show remarkable continuity from about 8,000 BP until today. It is only very recently, in the twentieth century in industrialising countries, that the peasant regime has been transformed into an industrial agrarian mode of production. In less-industrialised regions, many aspects of the agrarian regime as it evolved thousands of years ago can still be witnessed.

The second great ecological regime transformation also had other great consequences for the social and individual regimes of those involved. The early agriculturists had to learn new forms of self-discipline. They could no longer consume all the available food, as gatherers and hunters usually do. Eating the seeds or exhausting the food supplies well before the next harvest would have spelled disaster. In addition, people had to adapt to the agricultural cycle, with all the inherent constraints, such as sowing, weeding and harvesting in the right seasons. This made it necessary to invent ways and means to determine the appropriate time for this type of work, particularly for seeding, but also for harvesting. Success in animal husbandry implied new forms of self-discipline, too. For example, the people had to learn how to main-

64

tain growing herds of cattle, and not to slaughter their animals at will. More than before, people had to learn to think ahead as well as to restrain themselves. These new standards of conduct were not inborn, they had to be learned. In the same period, the early agriculturalists began abandoning the gatherer-hunter regime, particularly the need to follow the seasonal patterns of change exhibited by wild plants and animals. Thus, some relaxation of behaviourial standards, of the gatherer-hunter ecological regime, was taking place, too. This was possible because the problems associated with this regime gradually disappeared.

The need for these new forms of discipline was at least partially expressed through religion. The only plausible theory I know of which explains the origins of 'priesthood' and the rise of organised religion in early agrarian societies was formulated by Johan Goudsblom (Goudsblom et al. 1989:70-78). In turn, Goudsblom was inspired by the first two chapters of McNeill's *The Rise of the West* (1991:18-22, 33-40). Goudsblom's theory can be summarised as follows. As Norbert Elias argued, forms of self-constraint can only be properly understood in connection with external constraint (1982:229-333). This would also have applied to the need to adapt to the agrarian regime. This provided the emergent leaders with new power chances. They may have taken the lead in instilling the new standards of conduct with the aid of ritual and, by so doing, provided binding solutions to the social problems resulting from the transition to agriculture.

In my view the latter aspect, the need for binding solutions to the problems of production, storage and distribution as well as the solving of conflicts among sedentary human groups which were larger than ever before, was of particular importance for the successful introduction of an agrarian regime led by 'priest-chiefs' (cf. Spier 1994). Not all early agriculturists may have needed the priestly predictions resulting from celestial or biological observations or the disciplinary measures imposed by them. I think that those intelligent early agriculturists who, for instance, wished to foretell the turn of the seasons, could have made successful predictions by observing various other aspects of nature, such as the flowering of certain plants, the occurrence and behaviour of specific animals, etc. as many of them still do today. This argument also applies to the disciplinary aspects of the agrarian regime.

65

However, agricultural success presupposed the cooperation of a considerable number of people, including those who were perhaps not so talented as well as those who may have presented early examples of the 'free rider' problem. As a consequence, the solution of internal conflicts may have played an increasingly important role in such ritual.

To conclude, the need for agrarian discipline and social coordination on a scale larger than ever before required a form of leadership stronger than had been known previously. I think that largely for the reasons mentioned above agrarian behaviourial standards were expressed in a religious idiom to a considerable extent. This became the major power base of the emerging 'priest-chiefs'. The religious vocabulary was probably expressed in terms of non-human nature, and almost everywhere included a divine Earth, Sun, Moon, Thunder, etc., all the result of the strong dependency on the surrounding natural environment and its precarious nature.

These developments found a remarkable material expression in the temple mounds which were, for instance, constructed both by early Sumerians and Peruvians as part of the process of early state formation. Yet one may wonder to what extent the still remaining examples of these ritual structures were built with the exclusive aim of maintaining the agrarian regime. It may not be exaggerated to suggest that by the time such constructions came into existence, they served first of all to express and bolster the growing power and prestige of the society which built them as well as, and perhaps especially so, the status of its 'priesthood-*cum*-chieftaincy' (cf. Burger 1992:37-38). Their more humble predecessors may have led agrarian rites, including the determination of time, which were primarily executed to serve locally felt religious needs. Such rites would have been less elaborate and, as a consequence, may have left few archaeological traces. The remains of some early agricultural villages include sites that are interpreted as shrines, which suggests that by that time, the first rise of organised religion was taking place. It appears likely that most, if not all of the first priest-chiefs were men. If so, these developments contributed to the emergence of the male-dominated public domain.

66

AGRARIAN SOCIAL REGIME DIFFERENTIATION AND DEVELOPMENT

The agrarian way of life allowed a greater degree of social regime differentiation and development than ever before. While gatherer-hunter bands never evolved beyond the tribal stage, in the course of time the transition to an agrarian regime led to the formation of state societies for the first time in human history. However, these developments did not take place as soon as agricultural societies came into being. On the contrary, for thousands of years the landscape remained dotted with small, relatively autonomous peasant villages which were not subjected to any form of central control. State formation was a possibility contained within the agricultural regime, but not an automatic consequence.

The emergence of states, about 5,000 years BP, led to a growing diversity of social regimes worldwide. While in many regions people continued to make a living by gathering and hunting food and in other areas tribal societies engaged in animal husbandry or sedentary agriculture, complex societies began to arise in their midst. These states became more powerful than all the other social regimes around them and, as a result, influenced their neighbours to a much greater extent than vice versa.

Early states came into being from about 5,000 BP in many areas around the world. In most, if not all cases, both internal and external developments were responsible for the process of state formation. However, it needs to be emphasised that only the very first states arose without any influence from other, already existing, states. The formation of these pristine states, in both the Old and the New World, was therefore a fundamentally new development. In this case, too, Goudsblom's simple stage model is illuminating.

No society can be seen as providing the standard model for early state formation. For instance, the emergence of pristine states in two different regions that are usually considered unconnected during this period, the Middle East and Andean Peru, began differently but then converged to a strikingly similar pattern. This has, to my knowledge not yet been sufficiently recognised (cf. Fiedel 1992:356-362).

In the Middle East, the harvesting of wild cereals in mountainous areas seems to have preceded the cultivation of domesticated varieties in the same area from about 10,000 BP. Animals were tamed for meat, milk, and later for ploughing. The precursors of the first-known city states, which arose not in the mountains but along the coastline of what was becoming the 'Gulf', by contrast, seem to have relied on marine resources to a considerable extent. This provided their staple food for some millennia, while in the hinterland agriculture was becoming firmly established. After perhaps as long as 5,000 years, coastal societies situated near or along river banks began to develop irrigation agriculture coupled with animal husbandry, which led to the more familiar picture of 'hydraulic' early states (cf. Jacobson 1988).

In Andean Peru, both edible species such as tubers and fibres for clothing were cultivated from perhaps as early as 10,000 BP, also first in the mountains. Yet "plant and animal tending in the Cordillera served a secondary role, complementing other ways to make a living for thousands of years before it played a primary role as economic mainstay" (Moseley 1992:97). Along the desert coast, sedentary societies living in river valleys long remained dependent on sea food while they slowly introduced cultivated products as a supplement to their marine diet. From about 4,000 BP, early states in fertile valleys based on irrigation agriculture began to develop along the coast (Cohen 1977:265, Moseley 1975, 1992) and became increasingly similar to the early Mesopotamian city states. A similar pattern could be observed in early China (P.T. Ho, referred to in: Cohen 1977:154).

The arguments about the rising sea level put forward by Kennett and Kennett may lead to a reappraisal of the mechanism behind the emergence of early states, both in the Middle East and along the western Pacific coast of South America. For instance, after the last glacial period, which ended c.10,000 years ago, the Pacific coastline of Peru receded some 10 km inland (Chauchat 1988:59), while in the same period the Arabo/Persian Gulf became flooded. In these areas, the first early states arose. Little is known about their early stages of development. This is partially the result of a lack of systematic attention to such sites on dry land, but also because some of these areas are now flooded (cf. Jacobson 1988:72, Kennett & Kennett 1994). Thus, I would suggest that in order to better understand both early state formation and the developments which preceded it, we need to look underwater. There may well have been a comparatively long incipient stage toward early state formation which has until now remained obscured.

US marine geologists Daniel Stanley and Andrew Warne have suggested that when the sea level rise began to slacken off between 8500 and 7500 BP, this allowed the deposition of river sediments in such a way that fertile deltas were created at the mouth of rivers throughout the world such as the Nile, Rhone and Ebro in the Mediterranean, the Mississippi in North America, and the Yangtze (Chang Jiang) in China; and, I would suspect, also the Yellow river, along and above whose borders Chinese civilisation first emerged. This, in turn, first stimulated forms of (perhaps primitive irrigation) agriculture, and later the rise of civilizations in some of these regions (1993:435-438). The same argument would also be applicable, for instance, to the Pacific coastline of South America. If true, it would represent another interplay between natural and human regimes. However, perhaps like the rise of the Indus valley city states, the first known complex Chinese societies originated later and farther inland than those in Mesopotamia and Egypt, which makes it less probable that the emergence of the early Indus and Chinese urban civilisations was strongly affected by sea level rise.

In a perhaps even more provocative hypothesis, Douglas and James Kennett have suggested that varying ecological circumstances within which such floodplains formed may have affected the timing of the rise of early civilizations. Prior to inundation, the 'Gulf' was a shallow flat valley and later a shallow sea in which floodplains could easily develop at a rapid rate. The Nile river, by contrast, discharged its sediments directly into the deeper and steeper continental margin of the Mediterranean. This decreased the rate at which extensive floodplains formed in the delta. Only after the sea level had begun to stabilise could such fertile land be formed, somewhat later than the riverine borders of Mesopotamia, where the rapid marine transgression led to increasing competition for resources and, as a consequence, to cultural innovations. This time lag closely corresponds with the fact that Mesopotamian civilisation began to flourish earlier than its Egyptian counterpart.

In my view, a similar argument may at least partially explain the timing behind the origin of early Peruvian coastal states, and perhaps the comparatively late blossoming of early Chinese civilisation as well. The case of the Yangtze and Yellow rivers is more complicated because neither was surrounded by deserts. They were less circumscribed, in the words of US ethnologist Robert Carneiro (1970), which would have led to less severe constraints on the population for a considerable time than in the other centres where early states began to emerge.

In addition, it seems that during the period of early state formation in Mesopotamia, rainfall patterns began to change. The fertile river valleys received less rain, which increased the need for irrigation and, consequently, for central control. It may well be that societies with priest-chiefs advocating naturalistic religious views and practices which could contribute to efficiently tackling such problems were in an advantageous position. This may well have contributed to the rise of early states in Mesopotamia. Without more information it is impossible to say whether such an explanation would also be applicable to coastal Peru and/or other regions.

The increasing material possessions, a result of the transition to agriculture, would have contributed to the need for organised defence. In contrast to gatherers and hunters, who preferred to run and hide when threatened, the early agriculturalists had to defend themselves against attacks, tied as they had become to their possessions. This would have reinforced the need for leadership and organisation. It appears that in the first stages of agricultural development, religious and secular leadership were in all likelihood not differentiated, but were exercised by the same elite, whose leaders should therefore be characterised as priest-chiefs (cf. Goudsblom 1989:70-71, 89-90, Mann 1987:45-49). Both the early Mesopotamian and Peruvian agriculturists lived in "religious-agrarian" societies, to use Goudsblom's term (1989:80).

Rising material production also meant more garbage. Gatherers and hunters usually produced very little refuse. As US garbologist William Rathje and journalist Cullen Murphy explained:

> Throughout most of time human beings disposed of garbage in a very convenient manner: simply by leaving it where it fell. To be sure, they sometimes tidied up their sleeping and activity areas, but that was about all. Their disposal scheme functioned adequately because hunter-gatherers frequently abandoned their campgrounds to follow game or find new stands of plants (and, of

course, because there weren't that many hunter-gatherers to begin with). [...] As such habits suggest, our species faced its first garbage crisis when human beings became sedentary animals. The archaeologist Gordon R. Willey, who in the late 1940s conducted in Peru the first extensive archaeological study of regional settlement patterns over time, has argued (only partly in jest) that *Homo sapiens* may have been propelled along the path of civilization by his need for a degree of organization sufficiently sophisticated, and a class structure suitably stratified, to make possible the disposal of mounting piles of debris (1992:32-33).

Especially in urban areas, where high concentrations of people produced ever more refuse, the garbage problem made itself increasingly felt and, as a consequence, a type of garbage regime evolved. People began dumping rubbish outside as well as inside cities. Again, I quote Rathje and Murphy:

> The archaeologist C.W. Blegen, who dug into Bronze Age Troy during the 1950s, found that the floors of its buildings had periodically become so littered with animal bones and small artifacts that "even the least squeamish household felt that something had to be done." This was normally accomplished, Blegen discovered "not by sweeping out the offensive accumulation, but by bringing in a good supply of fresh clean clay and spreading it out thickly to cover the noxious deposit. In many a house, as demonstrated by the clearly marked stratification, this process was repeated time after time until the level of the floor rose so high that it was necessary to raise the roof and rebuild the doorway." Eventually, of course, buildings had to be demolished altogether, the old mudbrick walls knocked in to serve as the foundations of new mudbrick buildings. Over time the ancient cities of the Middle East rose high above the surrounding plains on massive mounds, called *tells*, which contained the ascending remains of centuries, even millennia, of prior occupation (1992:34-35).

Over the course of time, urban garbage regimes were refined. However, during most of their history, cities would remain very dirty places, as judged by modern North Atlantic standards. "For thousands of years," Lewis Mumford wrote in *The City in History*, "city dwellers put up with defective often quite vile, sanitary arrangements, wallowing in rubbish and filth they certainly had the power to remove" (quoted in: Rathje & Murphy 1992:40-41).

The continuing population growth also implied that pressure on the land increased. Agriculture was intensified, which inevitably led to growing social pressures. Tensions between neighbours rose. In many places, fighting between groups or villages became endemic. Raids by nomads became more frequent. Fortified villages and towns began to appear. This militarisation process took place in many areas but, of course, did not happen everywhere simultaneously, in the same way or to the same extent.

The reasons behind it are not difficult to understand. Formulated in Goudsblom's terms, agrarian societies are both productive and vulnerable. The increasing social tensions stimulated the development of specialised warriors who were unproductive and destructive but ready to fight (1989:74, 79-92). Agrarian societies with specialised warriors had greater chances for survival than those without, similar to the way the early agrarian societies with 'priest-chiefs' had an advantage over those without them. The increasing mutual threats stimulated a division of labour between what became warrior-chiefs and more specialised priests, who became ideological specialists attempting to dominate, sometimes even monopolise, the cosmovision of the ordinary people. This was usually expressed in terms of what we would call the supernatural. However, imperial China and the more recent communist regimes offer examples of the emergence of state-ideological specialists who fostered a more mundane vision, although with strong utopian overtones. In my view, they fulfilled similar societal roles as their more heavenly oriented colleagues elsewhere and in earlier times.

As a result of this process, in many places kings and priests emerged as separate elites. They needed each other for defence, offence, the religious legitimisation of power and the disciplining of the population by military and ideological means. As a result, an antagonistic-cooperative relationship between rulers and priests began to take shape, which from then on would become a dominant theme in human history until just very recently. The differentiation between priests and chiefs has never been fully completed. As far as I know, there have been no cases in which the warrior chiefs, kings or emperors, fully abandoned all priestly roles.

In all the great military-agrarian states, the rulers' positions were ultimately based on a monopoly over the means of violence. Of course, this monopoly was never absolute, but at least sufficiently strong to suppress uprisings or ward off attacks by foreigners (cf. Sanderson 1995:56-57). When the royal monopoly over the means of violence collapsed under inside or outside pressure, the state ceased to exist.

All of this formed part of the growing social differences within early states. A new type of social regime had emerged. Increasing numbers of people became more dependent on other people, and less directly dependent on the surrounding natural environment. Kings and priests, traders and artisans were increasingly dealing with problems concerning interhuman relations, while they passed on to the peasants the pressures of the agrarian ecological regime. Thus, for the evolving higher and middle strata of society, the ecological regime began to disappear from view. The majority of the population, peasants, fishers and miners, continued to be directly involved in exploiting natural resources.

In all the larger and smaller empires, elites invariably looked down on the peasantry, as well as on the ecological regime they represented. Tilling the land and manual labour in general became occupations with a low distinctive value. The status hierarchy became increasingly expressed by ideas of cleanliness and dirt, or rather by the way people could avoid getting dirty hands. The degrees of cleanliness and social prestige became intimately linked, most notably in India, but also elsewhere. To this day, the ecological regime is viewed by those who do not work the land as a low status occupation. And social competition is still largely contested with the aid of material means.

This was also expressed in religion. In the great world empires that formed, moral religions became the prerogative of first the middle and later the higher strata of society, while the peasantry continued to express their local religion to a considerable extent in supernatural terms modelled on the surrounding natural environment, such as mountain spirits, mother earth, etc. (cf. Spier 1990, 1994b). Over the course of time, the 'social' regime of the middle strata, of traders and artisans, revolved to a considerable extent around economics. Courtly elites became preoccupied with etiquette, while priests undertook the teaching of ethics (cf. Goudsblom 1994:12).[7] I do not wish to imply that these were the only regimes such people formed part of, but that these regimes figured very prominently among them.

The increasing social differences led to growing competition for status and prestige, which was to a considerable extent expressed with the aid of material means. Access to scarce resources became an important way of showing off one's social position. These means included objects which were not readily available locally but were obtained through long-distance trade, which flourished as a result. Alternatively, the refinement of locally produced commodities could also express power and prestige. In both cases, the prestige value of such objects was largely derived from the value added by labour. What such objects expressed was, in fact, the power to command labour. Of course, combinations of both types of material expression were very common. In addition, the power to monopolise the possession and use of certain material means became another indication of one's social ranking.

As a result, economic and information exchanges, activities probably as old as humanity, intensified enormously after the beginning of the agrarianisation process. In addition to a great variety of local barter, this increasingly included long-distance trade in both prestige and consumer goods, especially when the latter could be transported by ships. In the course of time, this led to a spread of skills of various kinds and to a great expansion of both the agrarian regime and the capitalist market regime which, in their turn, influenced the development of state regimes and vice versa (cf. Frank & Gills 1993, McNeill 1995b, Rowling 1987, Wolf 1982).

These economic developments produced strained relations between rulers and traders. In order to stay in power, the royalty had to keep all their vassals in check. Merchants, however, are mobile by their very nature. The rulers needed traders for the products they could deliver and the wealth they generated, but always feared that they would lose their grip on them and that, as a consequence, the realm would fall apart. It is not surprising, therefore, that rulers everywhere continuously sought to curb and control traders. This contributed to preventing the emergence of a global capitalist trade network for a long time. In the words of US sociologist Stephen Sanderson:

in agrarian-coercive societies 'capitalism is always struggling to get out'. Merchants could be hemmed in here and there, could have their wealth expropriated by this and that bureaucratic elite, but they could not be denied forever. Gradually their economic power grew, until, some 4,500 years after the origins of the first states and quite probably the first genuine merchants, they were able to conquer and subdue the very kind of society that gave them birth. It wasn't easy and it took a long time, but eventually it happened. It happened first in Europe and Japan, but if it had not happened there it would have happened somewhere else at a later time (1995:175).

The worldwide capitalist mercantile expansion which took place in the past millennium was indeed a spectacular novel social regime transformation. It was, however, not an ecological regime transformation. The rapidly growing capitalist trade stepped up pressure on the existing ecological regimes which, in turn, contributed to the search for new ways of producing things. These efforts increased sharply when the Old and New Worlds became interlinked. Thus, in the course of time the mercantile social regime transformation would help trigger the third great ecological regime transformation, industrialisation.

Growing differentiation between larger and smaller military-agrarian states, agrarian and nomadic tribes and marginalised gatherers and hunters to the advantage of the first was a dominant trend from 5,000 BP onwards, both in the Old and the New World. It is unclear to what extent these two major land-masses were interlinked through human contacts. Another case for comparative isolation was Australia. Yet, whatever the degree of worldwide interconnections, during this period communication networks of various kinds greatly intensified within both 'Worlds'.

As a result of these developments, the balance between humans and disease-causing microparasites was shifted (McNeill 1986). A considerable part of the original parasitic human disease pool of equatorial Africa did not spread all over the Earth, bound as it was to the local ecological conditions and limited by the human travel conditions (this is now rapidly changing as a result of improving communications). By contrast, 'civilised' diseases resulting from frequent contacts between humans and domesticated animals or transmitted by 'civilisation followers' such as rats and lice began to wreak havoc on human concentrations, particularly in towns. Harbour cities linked by extended trade networks were especially vulnerable. As a result, large-scale epidemics began to rage when great empires developed, which, in turn, led to an increased resistance to such diseases. In the Americas, by contrast, where only very few animals had been domesticated, infectious diseases hardly developed, if at all. This was also connected to lower population concentrations, both men and beasts, and indicates that contacts between the New and the Old World cannot have been very frequent or intense.[8]

Before industrialisation began, the power differences between the various great empires of the Eurasian continent had not been very pronounced. This is well attested by the fact that none of these major empires could impose its will on any of the others. When, for instance, Marco Polo travelled through Asia in the thirteenth century, or when Vasco da Gama visited India about two centuries later, they returned rather impressed but not overawed by what they had witnessed. From about 1500 AD, European trading posts were established in parts of Asia. However, by that time the great Asian empires could not yet be conquered by Europeans.

The European explorers' trips led to the final interlinking of the world into one global social regime. The European expansion all over the globe beginning around 1450 AD can be understood only by taking into account the large-scale developments of human society as a whole within its planetary ecological context (cf. Flynn & Giráldez 1995, McNeill 1985, 1991, Reynolds 1982, Wallerstein 1974-1989). In particular the conquest of the Americas was accomplished with amazing ease. This was possible first of all because of the uneven balance of illnesses. Eurasian infective diseases wreaked havoc among Amerindians, while Europeans did not suffer likewise from any form of Mexican or Peruvian microparasitical revenge. Of course, in many cases Europeans had superior military technology (cf. McNeill 1984 & 1995b). However, this superiority mattered very little all along the black African coast, where tropical diseases prevented the Europeans from establishing themselves farther inland before the advent of modern hygiene and medicine. Even then, West Africa in particular was considered a "white man's grave", and to some extent it still is, as I almost experienced myself in 1981. The great empires of South and Southeast Asia could only be conquered effectively when technical superiority resulting from industrialisation tilted the balance of power decisively in favour of the Europeans. In those parts of the world, Europeans and locals were more or less on equal footing in terms of resistance to diseases.

While the West European subjugation of the Americas and the more or less coincident Russian expansion to the East both formed part of the spread of the agrarian regime over the globe and of some of the social regimes associated with it (most notably state domination and the expanding capitalist market economy), the European colonisation of Southeast Asia and Africa, by contrast, formed part of the expansion of the emerging industrial regime.

THE THIRD GREAT ECOLOGICAL REGIME TRANSFORMATION: THE TRANSITION TOWARD AN INDUSTRIAL REGIME

According to US scholar David Landes, "the Englishman of 1750 was closer in material things to Caesar's legionnaires than to his own great-grandchildren" (1969:5). The third large ecological regime transformation, industrialisation on the basis of the large-scale use of engines driven by fossil fuels, lay at the root of this remarkable discontinuity. In fact, the industrial transformation can be seen as an intensification of the fire regime (cf. Goudsblom 1992).

Because it happened so very recently and left such a great many traces, the emergence of the industrialisation process is known with a precision unattainable for the preceding two great ecological regime transformations. The introduction of the steam engine as improved by Scottish inventor James Watt, followed by steam turbines, internal combustion engines and nuclear power, led directly to an expansion of the production of goods and services hitherto unknown, first in industry and later also in agriculture and animal husbandry. Through industrialisation, military means became ever more efficient. The rapidly growing and intensifying means of long-distance communication would not have been possible either without an economy increasingly based on inanimate fuels. On an ever growing scale and at an ever increasing rate the world was turned into a provider of natural resources for industry and into a market for its products.

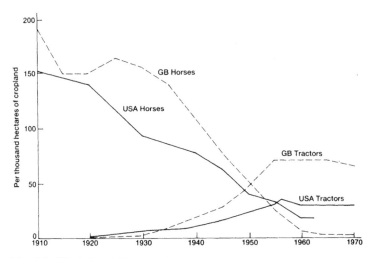

Fig. 4.3: *The industrialisation of agriculture as indexed by the numbers of horses and tractors per thousand hectares of cropland (from: Simmons 1994:240)*

The industrialisation of society could not have taken place without a long history of specific political, economic, socio-cultural, technical and scientific developments, most notably the first and second great ecological regime transformations as well as some of the social regime transformations associated with them, such as the formation of a regime of competing states and the associated drive for economic and military inventions. This is, however, not the place to summarise the academic discussion about this subject (see, for instance: Hobsbawn 1968, Landes 1969, Pollard 1992, Smil 1994, Stearns 1993, Wallerstein 1989).

Industrialisation began to gather speed first in Great Britain. But it did not take long before entrepreneurs and governments of many emerging nation-states, both in Europe and beyond, began to follow the British example by setting up modern industries. This was the beginning of the spread of industrialisation across the Earth, a process which has not yet been completed. Today, the early industrialising countries are all seeking to

78

maintain a lead, which provides the driving force for continuing industrial developments. Like the domestication of plants and animals and, undoubtedly, gathering and hunting, too, industrialisation is an ongoing process.

The third great ecological regime transformation can also be understood well with the aid of Goudsblom's simple phase model. Until today, the industrial mode of life has become dominant over all other forms of production, and has allowed those societies who have engaged in this adventure to become more powerful and wealthy than those who showed resistance to it. Of course, industrialisation has not been an unmitigated blessing. On the contrary, many people have suffered a great deal as a result of this transition. The point is simply that when some societies began to industrialise, the only options available to others were either to follow them or become marginalised.

As becoming part of the preceding major ecological regime transformations had made some cultural demands, industrialisation, too, implied learning new skills and new forms of self-discipline, which can be summarised as the 'industrial regime'. For instance, people had to learn to perform repetitive, often boring and sometimes potentially dangerous skills indoors for long hours. The need to efficiently run increasing numbers of factories led to a growing demand for social coordination. As a result, more than ever before, human life became regulated through clocks. Increasingly, daily material needs had to be purchased within a money economy and were no longer locally produced, sold or bartered. This tightening of the cultural screw went hand in hand with a relaxation of the agricultural regime for increasing numbers of people.

The coupling of ever refined techniques of information processing to machines driven by inanimate fuels can be interpreted as the secondary industrial revolution. It is the modern counterpart of the secondary agricultural revolution (the invention of the traction plough). This rather recent development has been gathering speed since the 1970s, and is currently bringing about incisive changes in the human social and ecological regimes. In North Atlantic societies, decreasing numbers of people are now working on the land or in factories while more and more humans spend most of their working days behind computer screens (including myself). This is to some extent caused by the globalisation of the industrial regime, which implies, among other things, that goods and services are increasingly produced all over the world. Labour-intensive manufacturing, in particular, has greatly diminished in the early industrialising countries, and it appears that information processing is now going the same way.

SOCIAL REGIME TRANSFORMATIONS

Industrialisation on the basis of inanimate fuels led to incisive worldwide social regime transformations. From a country in which the majority of the population worked and lived in the countryside, the United Kingdom was transformed into a largely urban society. As a result of its growing industrial potential, the United Kingdom succeeded in gaining a dominant position with regard to the surrounding nations. This was expressed in politi-cal and economic ways as well as in a socio-cultural sense. In many parts of the world, Great Britain strengthened its position, so that at the climax of its expansion, the peoples living on about a quar-ter of the surface of the planet had become incorporated into the British Empire. Many other parts of the globe which were not dominated politically became economically geared to British industry.

Industrialisation allowed and stimulated the expansion and further development of some existing social regimes, most notably population growth, state formation and development, and the spread of the market economy. The phenomenal growth of the world population needs no further comment. Nation-states spread all over the inhabitable Earth for the first time in human history, while in the twentieth century, the first worldwide organ-isations began to appear on the planetary stage.

The capitalist market regime both spread and intensified. It proved dominant over all other forms of economic exchange. Over the course of time, this led to growing wealth for increas-ing numbers of people, at least in the industrialising countries. The economic developments in human history can be charac-terised in the general terms of what British economist E.L. Jones has called "extensive" and "intensive" economic growth (Gouds-blom et al. 1989). Extensive growth indicates an increase of eco-nomic transactions as a result of population growth, while society as a whole does not get any richer. Intensive growth points at increasing wealth *per capita*. Although it is difficult to say to what extent extensive growth has been the dominant experience in human history, there can be no doubt that after 1945, in particular, industrialisation made possible intensive economic growth on a scale previously unequalled.

All these developments are closely related to the rapidly growing and intensifying communication networks of various kinds. They are increasingly making the world shrink, at least in the human experience. As a result, a type of global, or transnational, social regime is currently forming almost everywhere to a greater or lesser extent (cf. Mazlish & Buultjes 1993, de Swaan 1994), especially for city dwellers. Most notably during the twentieth century, urban concentrations have been growing at a rate greater than ever before, especially in the less industrialised countries. Thanks to improving health care, big cities are no longer death traps for impoverished peasants or enterprising youngsters, who have migrated in large numbers from the countryside. Poor they may be, yet many of them own radio and television sets, the proverbial 'windows on the world'. As a result, the great metropolitan areas of the world are all becoming part of one single global socio-cultural regime.

PLANETARY ECOLOGICAL REGIME DEVELOPMENT

All these developments have contributed to a massive rearrangement of the earthly biological regime. A great many plant and animal species are spreading to all planetary niches in which they may prosper. Often they were brought there by conscious human action, but also, and perhaps more frequently, inadvertently. To take only one example, the common practice in the shipping world of taking in ballast water along the coast of one continent and discharging it along the shores of another has very much contributed to the spread worldwide of smaller marine species. This, in turn, has led to efforts to counter or prevent such trends (Anderson 1992:12-13, 1993:5). According to a recent estimate by a study for the US Congress, the damage caused by unwelcome invaders of various kinds have cost the U.S.A. at least $97 billion this century (Kiernan 1993:9).

Photographs taken from trips to the Moon have greatly contributed to a feeling of human interdependence, as well as to a growing awareness of possible deleterious effects of human action on the planetary regime.[9] This includes fears of a growing hole in the ozone layer and the coming, or perhaps already existing, greenhouse effect, both of which are unintended results of human action. However, also on national and regional levels, the human impact on the natural environment is increasing. Today, for instance, the pace of natural geological change in the U.S.A. appears to be outdone by the rapid metamorphosis of the landscape through human enterprise. US geologist Roger Hooke claimed that:

> mining, road building, and construction of homes sift roughly 7.6 billion tonnes of soil a year in the US. By comparison, [US] rivers, the most important natural agents, transport only about 1 billion tonnes each year, if you ignore sediment dumped into them by human activity (quoted in: New Scientist 4 March 1995:11).

Also, nearby space is being increasingly affected by human behaviour. As a result of space exploration, lower earth orbits are filling up with all kinds of leftovers, ranging from lost screwdrivers via uncountable numbers of fragments from exploded rockets to burnt-out upper stages. Concern is rising that collisions between all these remnants may result in growing amounts of space debris circling the Earth which, in turn, would pose serious hazards to further space exploration. Humans have also left their marks on the Moon, and even on some planets, imprints which will probably remain there for longer than humanity itself exists.

Until recently, the opportunities industrialisation offered, as well as the fact that increasing numbers of people went to live in large urban concentrations and no longer tilled the land, contributed to a growing feeling of independence with regard to the natural environment. In other words, for those people the human ecological regime had further disappeared from view. Until recently this led to an almost total disregard for ecological problems, even among most academics.

The re-emergence of a generalised awareness of the importance of the human ecological regime was caused by the emergence of new problems. Growing pollution, the fear of exhausting natural resources considered essential, rapidly expanding garbage dumps, the extinction of growing numbers of natural species and, more recently, the possibility of altering whole ecosystems all contributed to the current rise of a new type of ecological regime, namely that of people who are not directly dependent on the natural environment, but who nevertheless are becoming aware that their actions do have an import on it. For this type of regime, which is new in the history of humanity, I propose the term 'environmental regime' (cf. Spier 1995a). It includes efforts as wide-ranging as coordinating human action on a global scale to prevent a possible greenhouse effect, countering acid rain, saving panda bears from extinction and separating household refuse.

Of course, environmental degradation caused by human action is not at all new, but is probably as old as humanity itself (cf. Ponting 1992, Simmons 1993, Spier 1992). Although in the deep past the deleterious effects were probably only locally felt, if they were recognised at all, from at least 2,000 BP some results of human enterprise had far-reaching effects. For instance, by examining samples from a Greenland ice core, an international team led by French geophysicist Claude Boutron has calculated that as a result of lead smelting in Greco-Roman antiquity over 800 years, a total of 400 tonnes of lead reached Greenland by air, where it was deposited in ice layers. This would have amounted to:

> about 15 percent of that caused by the massive use of lead alkyl additives in gasoline since the 1930s. Pronounced lead pollution is also observed during Medieval and Renaissance times. [...] This occurrence marks the oldest large-scale hemispheric pollution ever reported (Hong et al. 1994:1841).

However, the present levels of human-induced environmental change are unprecedented.

Summary and conclusions

About to enter the twenty-first century, humankind is experiencing an unparalleled degree of interlinking, as well as a growing feeling of vulnerability. Knowledge levels are higher than ever before, too. For instance, we are now able to work out our position within the history of the Universe, the galaxies, the Solar System, life on Earth, and that of our own species with an amount of precision and detail which even our recent ancestors would not have imagined possible.

In a variation of its original meaning, the term regime appears useful to describe all of cosmic history, including human history, ranging from the very large to the very small scale, as well as for analysing the interactions between all those levels, from micro- to macroprocesses. It provides an intellectual framework that helps to highlight similarities between the various aspects of history, some of which were not as clear to me before I undertook this enterprise as they are now.

Just because of its comparative vagueness and emptiness, the term regime appears to be more suitable as a general structuring term than other candidates, such as system and pattern, terms which are used as structuring principles with unqualified success in some sciences but are rejected in other scholarly circles. By contrast, the term regime appears acceptable to all branches of academe.

In no way should the analysis presented above be regarded as a comprehensive history of the Universe, the galaxies, Solar System, Earth, life, or humanity. Specialists will perhaps be quick to point out major omissions. Yet I would argue that this matters very little within the context of this analysis, which first of all aims to provide an intellectual framework for structuring big history. As long as the developments that others find lacking can be fitted into this general picture without major difficulties, and as long as the frame itself is not torn down, I will be more than happy.

While the structuring of cosmic, planetary and biological history with the aid of the term regime may meet little academic resistance – at least it proved to be by far the easiest part to structure in our course in big history –, structuring the history of our own kind is more contentious, since no widely accepted paradigm exists as yet. For this reason, I have devoted a great deal of space and attention to that comparatively tiny part of big history.

The history of humanity can be structured by referring to the three great ecological regime transformations which have taken place so far: the domestication of fire, the domestication of plants and animals, and industrialisation on the basis of engines driven by inanimate energy. As far as we know, only the second major transformation, the emergence of the agrarian regime, appears to have been at least partially caused by global climate change. However, evidence may also emerge for a connection between the original domestication of fire and environmental change. Industrialisation, by contrast, does not seem to have been influenced by such factors. Within and between these major stages, important social regime transformations can be recognised, such as sedentism, market formation, urbanisation, state formation, mercantile capitalist expansion, etc. All these large-scale developments led to continuous changes between and within societies, usually in the direction of growing numbers of people, and of increasing social differentiation and complexity.

A more detailed and refined structuring scheme of human history would inevitably involve paying more attention to smaller-scale social and ecological regime developments. Designing such a structure will not be a difficult task, because many scholars have already made important suggestions in this respect. Only an all-embracing paradigm for human history is still lacking.

The introduction of the agrarian regime and later the industrial regime allowed for the increasing differentiation and development of the social regimes. State and market formation and development led to growing power differentials between states, tribes and bands. In some societies, increasing room appeared for the emergence of individual regimes. This process is known as individualisation.

All the three great ecological regime transformations implied increasing power differentials. Almost without exception,

86

agrarian societies became more powerful than gatherers and hunters. The same can be said about the differences between industrialising societies and agrarian societies and, of course, of those with or without fire control. Also, the differentiation between social regimes led to power differentials.

Here we meet another important criterion for the structuring of human history, namely phase differentials and the resulting power differentials. The developing phase differentials provide a better way of structuring human history than looking only at their 'outcomes', the dominant human ecological and social regimes. As a result of these transformations, the mutual dependency relations between and within human, animal, floral and even the inanimate aspects of the planetary regime continuously shifted, at an accelerating pace.

By viewing human history as taking place between micro- and macroprocesses and the associated regimes, we can observe the following. Although humans have remained completely dependent on the general 'laws' that govern microprocesses, they have increasingly learned to manipulate such processes to their own benefit, at least in the short term. Influencing most of the macroprocesses, however, from plate tectonics to the movements of the celestial bodies, is still beyond human reach. However, the growth in human numbers and the effects of the intensifying human ecological regime, including the manipulation of microprocesses, are increasingly influencing the planetary regime, although to an extent yet unknown. For the first time in human history, this stage has been reached.

In summary, all aspects of nature can be viewed as regimes of varying sizes and shapes. Their mutual relations should be seen in terms of balances of influence. I hope that this way of looking at big history may not only provide a fruitful way of looking at our common past but also be helpful in dealing with the problems we are facing today.

Notes

1   For an extensive overview (in Dutch) of efforts made by a great
    variety of scholars and lay people to structure human history
    until about 1950 see: van der Pot 1951. See also: Green 1992.
2   In this century: Norbert Elias, Andre Gunder Frank, Marvin
    Harris, Michael Mann, Talcott Parsons, Marshall Sahlins,
    Stephen Sanderson, Elman Service, Julian Steward, Immanuel
    Wallerstein, Max Weber, Leslie White, Eric Wolf; in the nine-
    teenth century: August Comte, Karl Marx, Lewis Henry Mor-
    gan, Herbert Spencer.
3   For instance: Ardey 1969, Darlington 1969, L. & F. Cavalli-
    Sforza 1995.
4   For a recent overview of largely pre-human history by out-
    standing specialists see: *Scientific American*, October 1994.
5   Fernand Braudel's structuring scheme of *longue durée*, *conjoncture*
    and *événement* corresponds with the subdivision of ecological,
    social and individual regimes to a considerable extent (1966).
    Braudel's emphasis on the remarkable continuity of ecological-
    geographical aspects, the *longue durée*, during the period of
    Mediterranean history he studied is, of course, illuminating.
    This does not mean that ecological regimes are always stable.
    Braudel's analysis did not span a sufficiently long period to
    include major ecological regime transformations, such as the rise
    of agriculture or industrialisation (see: chapters three and four).
    This is a major reason why Braudel's terms are less suitable for
    the analysis of human history as a whole.
6   In fact, the Schrödinger equation provides the basis for two
    competing, mutually exclusive, general models of micro-
    processes. The established form of quantum mechanics, known
    as the Copenhagen interpretation, is built entirely on chance
    calculations. However, a little-known rival general theory of
    microprocesses exists, championed by Louis de Broglie and
    David Bohm, which retains some degree of determinism as well
    as cause and effect, and would accommodate the existing factual

knowledge just as well. For some reason, at least partially of socio-political nature, this theory has not (yet) become part of mainstream physics (Cushing 1994, Horgan 1993).

7   The concept of relative autonomy of higher levels of complexity and the corresponding decreasing levels of generality as the explanation for and legitimisation of relatively autonomous branches of science, such as biology and sociology, was probably first formulated by French sociologist Auguste Comte around 1830 (cf. Heilbron 1995:223 ff.). Norbert Elias has also emphasised this theme (1978a:45 ff.). With every higher level of relative autonomy and thus of complexity of the phenomena studied, quantitative approaches become less practical and insightful, while the need for qualitative analysis increases.

CHAPTER II

1   Sir Isaac Newton was already aware of this. In his book *Opticks*, he defended the notion that God's influence was behind the regular planetary orbits by saying: "For while Comets move in very eccentrick Orbs in all manner of positions, blind Fate could never make all the Planets move one and the same way in Orbs concentrick, some inconsiderable irregularities excepted, which may have risen from the mutual Actions of Comets and Planets upon one another, and which will be apt to increase, till this System wants a Reformation" (1979:402). This problem has occupied the minds of astronomers ever since, but the 'perturbation calculations' were usually too difficult to tackle mathematically before supercomputers and modern chaos theory appeared (cf. Peterson 1995).

2   It is thought that the asteroid belt did not merge into one single planet because the gravitational force exerted by Jupiter prevented this from happening. It would have torn apart any larger proto-planetary chunks that had formed.

3   It is remarkable that Kauffman uses both the terms 'system' and 'regime' without, however, providing any definitions. His understanding of regimes appears to be identical to mine.

CHAPTER III

1   It is no coincidence that of all the disciplines within the humanities, the archaeological profession devotes the most systematic attention to ecological circumstances in relation to cultural developments. In comparison with most historians, anthropologists and sociologists, archaeologists often deal with long-term developments of societies that, more than their modern counterparts, were subjected to the vagaries of nature as a result of the prevailing human ecological regimes.

2   It could be argued that there were two stages (no one has 'it' and some have 'it') before all people engaged in hunting and gathering. In Africa, ancient hominids appear to have made a living by scavenging carcasses killed by large carnivores (Gamble 1995:66-70). For lack of evidence it is impossible to say to what extent the early folk added plants to their diet.

CHAPTER IV

1   O'Hanlon went on to argue that modern attempts at preventing forest fires lead to growing chances of large-scale fires that are increasingly difficult to control, while these efforts also upset the established balances in the ecosystem.

2   A cursory inspection of archaeological textbooks has yielded the following. The handbook by the British archaeologists Colin Renfrew and Paul Bahn (1991), generally considered authoritative, pays considerable attention to changing ecological circumstances, but does not make any references to a possible need to reconsider our image of early humankind in view of these developments. This may indicate that at least until recently, among archaeologists this problem was not recognised in a general sense. However, in all the regional overviews I have consulted so far, which include the Americas, Europe, the Middle East and Korea, this problem has received some attention. Some specialists have pointed to this possibility for the region covered by the book or quoted scholars who had made such suggestions; others hypothesised that various forms of environmental change are among the reasons why the archaeological record does not provide an accurate picture of the regional past; while others at least

pointed to a substantial rise of the sea level. For the Americas: Bruhns 1994:43, Burger 1992:35, 68, Chauchat 1988:59, Fiedel 1992:84, 168, 170, Moseley 1992:99; for Europe: Cunliffe 1994:16-19, 44-45, 81-89; for the Middle East: Ben-Tor 1992:14, Jacobson 1988:72, Kennett & Kennett 1994, Stanley & Warne 1993; for Korea: Nelson 1993:59. See also: Roberts 1989, Stewart 1994. Mark Cohen (1977) dismissed the idea that sea-level rise would have obscured evidence of many early coastal societies. I think that he underestimated the importance of environmental change.

3   My experience with the study of world and human history has taught me that even well-established reference books, such as the *Times Atlas of World History* (Barraclough & Parker 1994) and the *Penguin Encyclopedia of Ancient Civilizations* (Cotterell 1988) sometimes show a clear bias towards emphasising the results of archaeological research on the Eurasian continent while seemingly ignoring the existing literature about the Americas, and perhaps about other areas as well. For instance, in these hand-books both the dating of the beginning of agriculture and of the rise of early states in the Americas are very inaccurate. According to authoritative sources these events took place a great deal earlier than mentioned. There is still a long way to go to reach a truly planetary perspective of history.

4   According to US archaeologist of Peru Michael Moseley, the great German traveller and natural scientist, Alexander von Humboldt, recognised this pattern already in the nineteenth century when visiting Andean Peru. "Aware that tens of thousands of plants and animals thrived, but that fewer than one per cent were domesticated, a notion of risk lay at the heart of his ideas. Von Humboldt believed that early experiments with tending organisms and altering their behaviour and characteristics offered far greater chances for failure than for success. Therefore, the origins of domestication would not be found among well-off people living in productive habitats because they had little reason to accept such risks. The motivation for tending wild resources would instead be found among the inhabitants of marginal settings and harsh environments. Here, confronted with low or insecure yields from nature, trial and error with the care of plants and animals offer acceptable risks as potential means of stabilizing or increasing food supplies. The Prussian scholar rea-

soned that people were gradually pushed into harsh settings conducive to experimentation as population growth filled more favorable habitats. [...] Von Humboldt saw necessity as the mother of invention, but his theory does not imply that people consciously sought to domesticate plants and animals. In the Andes, the major route to domestication lay with experiments that encouraged plants and animals inhabiting one place or zone to live in another. The motivation for altering the distribution of wild resources may have been to increase their numbers, as herders do when they irrigate bofedal pasture, or simply to bring them closer to where people lived. [...] Distances between natural occurrence and human placement were probably short to begin with. Yet, in the rugged Cordillera living conditions change over very short distances and habitats can vary within a few hundred meters of elevation. Therefore, moving organisms and altering their placement injected both human selection and natural selection into the Andean domestication process. Travelling the Cordillera, von Humboldt could see that the domestication process remained unending and that the harsh highlands were still undergoing agricultural and pastoral transformations in the nineteenth century, as they are today." (Moseley 1992:95). Von Humboldt's most interesting ideas about the transition to agriculture appear to be unknown among modern theorists of the agricultural revolution. Especially the role in early domestication of the varied ecological regime of mountains has not yet received the attention it deserves (cf. Redman 1978).

5   The British archaeologist Andrew Sherratt elaborated this argument (1981). He called these developments the "secondary products revolution".

6   The emergence of the veterinary profession as a result of these developments is the subject of a PhD thesis currently being prepared by British social scientist Jo Swabe at the Amsterdam School for Social Science Research.

7   Goudsblom perhaps very wisely restricted his typification to "European court society [...] at its peak". I think that his formulation may well be suitable to characterise many, if not all, military-agrarian societies.

8   The lack of resistance to 'civilised' diseases does not necessarily point to a complete absence of contacts. Even today, Amazonian tribes, for instance, are extremely vulnerable to infectious dis-

eases, notwithstanding the fact that these had been imported at least four centuries earlier, and had caused a massive extinction of local populations also in the Amazon region. Whatever kind of 'primitive' life modern Amazonian tribes may lead today, in no way should they be considered to have led a totally isolated existence until very recently. When contacts are sparse, diseases may simply not succeed in crossing societal frontiers, because those who carry the microparasites may well succumb to them (or vanquish them and become healthy) before they can transmit them.

9   The great emotional impact of photos of the Earth taken by Apollo astronauts makes me wonder to what extent the European expansion of the late fifteenth and early sixteenth centuries may have produced similar psychological effects. The discovery of the Americas brought about, among other things, a shockwave of fear, since people in Western Europe began to realise that the world was different than they had thought hitherto. While in this period world maps became in fact more reality congruent, they began to sport a variety of strange fearful animals and humanoids, both on land and in the oceans. The same phenomenon can be observed on sky maps, which also needed revision because a considerable part of the southern sky had not been seen by European eyes before that time. About a century later, West European maps had reached new levels of accuracy, and the strange beings then largely disappeared. Instead, these maps are surrounded by depictions of the peoples encountered by the European seafarers as well as by drawings of unfamiliar cities and landscapes. This reflected (perhaps unwittingly) the growing self-confidence of travellers and map makers. I think that the current attempts to view the Earth as one single system, as well as the efforts of thinking in terms of big history, are all aimed at producing new scientific 'maps' in order to regain our self-confidence. Thus, modern fears about an ecological catastrophe awaiting vulnerable Spaceship Earth caused by human action may partially have originated from a shock wave similar to that which pervaded West European societies about 500 years before. It is curious that personal observations play such a crucial role in these processes. The knowledge that the Earth is a globe swinging around the Sun in deep space was not new at all. In this context, it is curious that photos similar to the 'Awesome

Views from Apollo 8' had already been taken by the unmanned Lunar Orbiter-1 spacecraft in 1966. Although these pictures became famous, they never had anything near the emotional impact of the snapshots taken by living astronauts who had witnessed the view themselves. A similar phenomenon can be observed by looking at the art of map making as it developed worldwide during the past five centuries. Maps made in seventeenth-century Japan and China, for instance, nations which did not sail the seven seas but contented themselves with copying the results of others, did not express any fear of unknown parts of the world, at least not visibly. I will explore this theme elsewhere in more detail.

References

Allardyce, Gilbert
1990   'Toward World History: American Historians and the Coming of the World History Course.' *Journal of World History 1* 1 (23-76).

Andel, Tjeerd H. van
1994   *New Views on an Old Planet. A History of Global Change.* Cambridge, Cambridge University Press (1985).

Anderson, Ian
1992   'End of the line for deadly stowaways?' *New Scientist* 24 October (12-13).
1993   'Aliens slip through international "safety net".' *New Scientist* 3 July (5).

Ardey, Robert
1969   *The Territorial Imperative. A Personal Inquiry into the Animal Origins of Property and Nations.* London, Fontana (1967).

Arriaza, Bernardo
1995   'Chinchorro Mummies.' *National Geographic 187* 3 (68-90).

Barraclough, Geoffrey & Parker, Geoffrey (eds.)
1994   *The Times Atlas of World History.* London, HarperCollins, Times Books (1978).

Barrow, John D.
1994   *The Origin of the Universe.* London, Weidenfeld & Nicholson.

Bax, Mart
1982   '"Wie tegen de kerk piest wordt zelf nat", over uitbreiding en intensivering van het clericale regime in Noord-Brabant.' ('"Whoever pees against the church becomes wet." On the expansion and intensification of the clerical regime in North Brabant.') *Antropologische Verkenningen I* nr. 2 (20-58).
1983   'Religious Infighting and the Formation of a Dominant Catholic Regime in Southern Dutch Society.' *Social Compass 32* (57-72).

1985   'Popular Devotions, Power and Religious Regimes in Catholic Dutch Brabant.' *Ethnology 24* nr. 3 (215-227).
1987   'Religious Regimes and State Formation: Towards a Research Perspective.' *Anthropological Quarterly 60* 1 (1-11).
1995   *Medjugorje: Religion, Politics and Violence in Rural Bosnia.* Amsterdam, VU University Press.

Ben-Tor, Amnon (ed.)
1992   *The Archaeology of Ancient Israel.* New Haven & London, Yale University Press / The Open University of Israel.

Braudel, Fernand
1966   *La Méditerranée et le monde méditerranéen à l'époque de Philippe II,* 2e éd. revue et augmentée (2 vols.). Paris, Librairie Armand Colin (1949).

Bray, Warwick M., Swanson, Earl H. & Farrington, Ian S.
1989   *The Ancient Americas.* Oxford, Phaidon Press (1975).

Bruin, Jan, Sabelis, Maurice W. & Dicke, Marcel
1995   'Do plants tap SOS signals from their infested neighbours?' *Trends in Ecology and Evolution 10* nr. 4 (167-170).

Bruhns, Karen Olsen
1994   *Ancient South America.* Cambridge, Cambridge University Press.

Buckley, Ann
1994   'Music and Humanisation as a Long-Term Process.' In: Marcel Otte (ed.) *Sons Originels Préhistoire de la musique.* Université de Liège, (Belgium), E.R.A.U.L. 61.

Budiansky, Stephen
1992   *The Covenant of the Wild: Why Animals Chose Domestication.* New York, William Morrow.

Burger, Richard L.
1992   *Chavín and the Origins of Andean Civilization.* London, Thames and Hudson.

Carneiro, Robert L.
1970   'A theory of the origin of the state.' *Science 169* 3947 (733-738).

Cavalli-Sforza, Luca & Francesco
1995   *The Great Human Diaspora.* New York, Addison-Wesley.

Chauchat, Claude
1988   'Early hunter-gatherers on the Peruvian coast.' In: Richard W. Keatinge (ed.) *Peruvian Prehistory*. Cambridge, Cambridge University Press (41-67).

Christian, David
1991   'The Case for "Big History".' *Journal of World History 2* 2 (223-238).
1994   'Inner Eurasia as a Unit of World History.' *Journal of World History 5* 2 (173-212).

Cohen, Marc Nathan
1977   *The Food Crisis in Prehistory. Overpopulation and the Origins of Agriculture*. New Haven / London, Yale University Press.

Coppens, Yves
1994   'East Side Story: The Origin of Humankind.' *Scientific American 270* 11, May (62-69).

Costello, Paul
1993   *World Historians and Their Goals. Twentieth Century Answers to Modernism*. DeKalb, Northern Illinois Press.

Cotterell, Arthur (ed.)
1988   *The Penguin Encyclopedia of Ancient Civilizations*. Harmondsworth, Penguin Books (1980).

Crosby, Alfred W.
1972   *The Columbian Exchange. Biological and Cultural Consequences of 1492*. Westport, Conn., Greenwood Press.
1993   *Ecological Imperialism. The Biological Expansion of Europe, 900-1900*. Cambridge, Cambridge University Press (1986).

Croswell, Ken
1992   'Why intelligent life needs giant planets.' *New Scientist* 24 October (18).

Cunliffe, Barry (ed.)
1994   *The Oxford Illustrated Prehistory of Europe*. Oxford / New York, Oxford University Press.

Cushing, James T.
1994   *Quantum Mechanics: Historical Contingency and the Copenhagen Hegemony*. Chicago & London, University of Chicago Press.

Darlington, C.D.
1969   *The Evolution of Man and Society*. London, George Allen & Unwin.

Dayton, Leigh
1992   'Pacific islanders were world's first farmers.' *New Scientist* 12 December (14).

Drucker, Philip
1963   *Indians of the Northwest Coast*. Garden City, New York, The Natural History Press (1955).

Efrat, Barbara S. & Langlois, W.J. (eds.)
1978   *nu•tka• Captain Cook and The Spanish Explorers on the Coast*. Victoria, B.C., Aural History Provincial Archives of British Columbia.

Elias, Norbert
1978a   *What is Sociology?* London, Hutchinson.
1978b   *The History of Manners. The Civilizing Process: Volume I*. New York, Pantheon Books.
1982   *Power and Civility. The Civilizing Process: Volume II*. New York, Pantheon Books.
1987a   'The Retreat of Sociologists into the Present.' *Theory, Culture & Society 4* 2-3 (213-222).
1987b   *Involvement and Detachment*. Oxford, Basil Blackwell.
1992   *The Symbol Theory (edited with an introduction by Richard Kilminster)*. London etc., Sage Publications.

Fiedel, Stuart J.
1992   *Prehistory of the Americas, second edition*. Cambridge, Cambridge University Press (1987).

Flanagan, Ruth
1995   'Killer trees choked ocean life.' *New Scientist* 22 April (17).

Flynn, Dennis O. & Giráldez, Arturo
1995   'Born with a "Silver Spoon": The Origin of World Trade in 1571.' *Journal of World History 6* 2 (201-222).

Frank, Andre Gunder & Gills, Barry K.
1993   *The World System. Five hundred years or five thousand?* London & New York, Routledge.

Fung Pineda, Rosa
1988   'The Late Preceramic and Initial Period.' In: Richard W. Keatinge (ed.) *Peruvian Prehistory*. Cambridge, Cambridge University Press (67-99).

Gama, Vasco da
1986   *Die Entdeckung der Seewegs nach Indien*. Stuttgart, Erdmann.

Gamble, Clive
1995   *Timewalkers. The Prehistory of Global Colonization*. Harmondsworth, Penguin Books (1993).

Geiss, Imanuel
1993   *Geschichte griffbereit* (six volumes). Dortmund, Harenberg Lexicon-Verlag.

Gerritsen, Jan-Willem
1993   *De politieke economie van de roes* (The Political Economy of Intoxication). Amsterdam, Amsterdam University Press.

Gleick, James
1988   *Chaos: Making a New Science*. Harmondsworth, Penguin Books (1987).

Goudie, Andrew
1987   *The Human Impact on the Natural Environment, 4th edition*. Oxford, Basil Blackwell (1986).

Goudsblom, Johan
1977   *Sociology in the Balance*. Oxford, Basil Blackwell.
1990   'The Impact of the Domestication of Fire Upon the Balance of Power Between Human Groups and Other Animals.' *Focaal 13* (55-65).
1992   *Fire and Civilization*. London, Allen Lane.
1994   *The Theory of Civilizing Processes and Its Discontents*. Paper for the XIIIth World Congress of Sociology, 18-23 July 1994, Bielefeld, Germany, Ad Hoc Sessions on Figurational Sociology.

Goudsblom, Johan, Jones, E.L. & Mennell, Stephen
1989   *Human History and Social Process*. University of Exeter Press, Exeter Studies in History No. 26.

Gould, Stephen Jay
1989   *Wonderful Life: The Burgess Shale and the Nature of History*. New York, W.W. Norton & Company.

1994   'The Evolution of Life on the Earth.' *Scientific American* Vol. *271*
4 October (62-69).

Gould, Stephen Jay (ed.)
1993   *The Book of Life*. London, Ebury / Hutchinson.

Graedel, Thomas E. & Crutzen, Paul J.
1995   *Atmosphere, Climate and Change*. New York etc., W.H. Freeman
& Co., Scientific American Library.

Green, William A.
1992   'Periodization in European and World History.' *Journal of World
History 3* 1 (13-54).

Gribbin, John
1993   *In the Beginning. The Birth of the Living Universe*. London,
Viking.

Guillet, David
1983   'Towards a Cultural Ecology of Mountains: The Central Andes
and the Himalayas Compared.' *Current Anthropology 24* 5 (561-
674).

Gupta, Joyeeta, Junne, Gerd & Wurff, Richard van der
1993   *Determinants of Regime Formation*. University of Amsterdam,
Dept. of International Relations and Public International Law &
Vrije Universiteit Amsterdam, Institute of Environmental Studies, Working Paper 1.

Haas, Peter M.
1980   'Why Collaborate? Issue Linkage and International Regimes.'
World Politics 32 (357-405).
1989   'Do Regimes Matter? Epistemic communities and Mediterranean pollution control.' *International Organization 43* 3 (377-
403).

Hanks, Patrick, Mcleod, William T. & Urdang, Laurence
1986   *Collins Dictionary of the English Language, 2nd Ed.*. London &
Glasgow, Collins.

Harris, David R.
1990   *Settling Down and Breaking Ground: Rethinking the Neolithic Revolution*. Amsterdam, Stichting Nederlands Museum voor
Anthropologie en Praehistorie, Twaalfde Kroon-Voordracht.

Harris, Marvin
1975   *Culture, People, Nature. An Introduction to General Anthropology.* New York, Harper & Row.
1977   *Cannibals and Kings. The Origins of Cultures.* New York, Vintage Books.
1980   *Cultural Materialism: The Struggle for a Science of Culture.* New York, Vintage Books.

Hayes, Peter & Smith, Kirk (eds.)
1993   *The Global Greenhouse Regime: Who Pays? Science, Economics and North-South Politics in the Climate Change Convention.* London, Earthscan.

Hecht, Jeff
1994   'Is the solar system surrounded by relics of its past?' *New Scientist* 16 July (18).
1995a   'Nearby space "could not support life".' *New Scientist* 18 February (14-15).
1995b   'First sighting of Kuiper Belt comets.' *New Scientist* 18 May (19).

Heilbron, Johan
1995   *The Rise of Social Theory.* Oxford, Polity Press.

Heiser Jr., Charles B.
1990   *Seed to Civilization. The Story of Food.* Cambridge, Mass., Harvard University Press.

Hobsbawm, E.J.
1968   *Industry and Empire.* Harmondsworth, Penguin.

Hong, Sungmin, Candelone, Jean-Pierre, Patterson, Clair C. & Boutron, Claude F.
1994   'Greenland Ice Evidence of Hemispheric Lead Pollution Two Millennia Ago by Greek and Roman Civilizations.' *Science 265* (1841-1843).

Horgan, John
1993   'Last words of a quantum heretic.' *New Scientist* 27 February (38-42).

Jacobson, Thorkild
1988   'Sumer.' In: Arthur Cotterell (ed.) *The Penguin Encyclopedia of Ancient Civilizations.* Harmondsworth, Penguin Books.

Junne, G.
1992   'Beyond Regime Theory.' *Acta Politica 27* (9-28).

Kaler, James B.
1992   *Stars.* New York etc., W.H. Freeman & Co., Scientific American
Library.

Kauffman, Stuart
1995   *At Home in the Universe. The Search for Laws of Complexity.* London, Viking / the Penguin Press.

Kennett, Douglas J. & Kennett, James P.
1994   *Influence of Early Holocene Marine Transgression and Climate
Change on Human Cultural Evolution in Southern Mesopotamia.*
Marine Science Institute, University of California, Santa Barbara, 24 pp. (to be published).

Kiernan, Vincent
1993   'US counts cost of alien invaders.' *New Scientist* 23 October (9).

Kortlandt, Adriaan
1972   *New Perspectives on Ape and Human Evolution.* Amsterdam,
Stichting voor Psychobiologie.

Kortlandt, Adriaan vs. Coppens, Yves
1994   'Rift over Origins.' *Scientific American* Vol. *271* 4, October (5).

Krasner, Stephen D. (ed.)
1982   'International Regimes.' *International Organization* (special issue)
36 2.
1983   *International Regimes.* Ithaca & London, Cornell University
Press.

Landes, D.S.
1969   *The Unbound Prometheus: Technological change and industrial development in Western Europe from 1730 to the present.* Cambridge,
Cambridge University Press.

Lederman, Leon M. & Schramm, David M.
1995   *From Quarks to the Cosmos. Tools of Discovery.* New York etc., W.H.
Freeman & Co., Scientific American Library (1989).

Lehninger, Albert L.
1975   *Biochemistry. The Molecular Basis of Cell Structure and Function.
Second Edition.* New York, Worth Publishers.

Lewis, Henry T.
1972   'The Role of Fire in the Domestication of Plants and Animals in
Southwest Asia: A Hypothesis.' *Man 7* 2 (195-222).

Longair, Malcolm S.
1996   *Our Evolving Universe*. Cambridge, Cambridge University Press.

Lovelock, J.E.
1987   *Gaia: A new look at life on Earth*. Oxford, New York, Oxford University Press (1979).

Mann, Michael
1987   *The Sources of Social Power. Volume I: A history of power from the beginning to A.D. 1760*. Cambridge, Cambridge University Press.
1993   *The Sources of Social Power. Volume II: The rise of classes and nation-states, 1760-1914*. Cambridge, Cambridge University Press.

Matthews, Robert
1994   'The ghostly hand that spaced the planets.' *New Scientist* 9 April (13).

Mazlish, Bruce & Buultjes, Ralph
1993   *Conceptualizing Global History*. Boulder, Colorado etc., Westview Press.

McNeill, William H.
1974   *The Shape of European History*. New York etc., Oxford University Press.
1978   *The Metamorphosis of Greece since World War II*. Oxford, Basil Blackwell.
1984   *The Pursuit of Power. Technology, Armed Force and Society since AD 1000*. Chicago, University of Chicago Press (1982).
1985   *Plagues and Peoples*. Harmondsworth, Penguin books (1976).
1986a   'Organizing Concepts for World History.' *Review* X 2 (211-229).
1986b   *History of Western Civilization. A Handbook*. Chicago, University of Chicago Press (1949).
1991   *The Rise of the West. A history of the human community; with a retrospective essay*. Chicago, University of Chicago Press (1963).
1992   *The Global Condition. Conquerors, Catastrophes and Community*. Princeton, Princeton University Press.
1993a   *A History of the Human Community. Prehistory to the Present*. Englewood Cliffs, New Jersey, Prentice-Hall (1963).
1993b   'Foreword.' In: Andre Gunder Frank & Barry K. Gills (eds.) *The World System. Five hundred years or five thousand?* London & New York, Routledge.
1994   *Reason and Violence*. Princeton University, Center of International Studies, Monograph Series Number 2.

1995a   *Keeping Together in Time. Dance and Drill in Human History.* Cambridge, Mass., Harvard University Press.

1995b   *Information and Transport Nets in World History.* Paper prepared for the Lund Conference on World System History, 25-28 March 1995.

Mennell, Stephen
1989   *Norbert Elias. Civilization and the Human Self-image.* Oxford, Basil Blackwell.

Moore, Walter J.
1968   *Physical Chemistry (fourth edition).* London, Longmans Green and Co Ltd. (1962).

Morrison, Philip & Phylis
1994   *Powers of Ten. About the Relative Size of Things in the Universe.* New York etc., W.H. Freeman & Co., Scientific American Library (1982).

Moseley, Michael Edward
1975   *The Maritime Foundations of Andean Civilization.* Menlo Park, Ca., Cummings Publishing Company.
1992   *The Incas and Their Ancestors. The Archaeology of Peru.* London, Thames and Hudson.

Murra, John V.
1975   *Formaciones económicas y políticas del mundo andino.* Lima, Instituto de Estudios Peruanos.

Murray, Bruce
1989   *Journey into Space. The First Three Decades of Space Exploration.* New York, London, W.W. Norton & Co.

Nelson, Sarah Milledge
1993   *The Archaeology of Korea.* Cambridge, Cambridge University Press.

Newton, Sir Isaac
1979   *Opticks.* New York, Dover Publications (1730).

O'Hanlon, Larry
1995   'Fighting Fire with Fire.' *New Scientist* 15 July (28-34).

Osborne, Roger & Tarling, Don
1995   *The Viking Historical Atlas of the Earth.* Harmondsworth, Penguin Books.

Pain, Stephanie
1993   'Modern hunter-gatherers no guide to Stone Age past.' *New Scientist* 20 February (8).
1994   "Rigid' cultures caught out by climate change.' *New Scientist* 5 March (13).

Parsons, Talcott
1977   *The Evolution of Societies*. Englewood Cliff, N.J., Prentice-Hall.

Pennisi, Elizabeth
1995   'The Secret Language of Bacteria.' *New Scientist* 16 September (30-33).

Peterson, Ivars
1995   *Newton's Clock. Chaos in the Solar System*. New York, W.H. Freeman and Company (1993).

Picard, Bernard
1723   *Ceremonies et coutumes religieuses de tous les peuples du monde. Tome Premier. Qui contient les ceremonies des Juifs & des Crétiens Catholiques*. Amsterdam, J.F. Bernard.

Pollard, Sidney
1992   *Peaceful Conquest. The Industrialization of Europe 1760-1970*. New York etc., Oxford University Press (1981).

Polo, Marco
1993   *The Travels of Marco Polo; The Complete Yule-Cordier Edition (two vols.)*. New York, Dover Publications (1920).

Ponting, Clive
1992   *A Green History of the World*. Harmondsworth, Penguin Books (1991).

Pot, J.H.J. van der
1950   *De periodisering der geschiedenis. Een overzicht der theorieën. Met een voorwoord van prof. dr J.M. Romein*. (The Periodisation of History. An overview of theories. with a foreword by Prof. Dr. J.M. Romein). The Hague, Uitgeverij W.P. van Stockum en Zoon.

Priem, Harry N.A.
1993   *Aarde en Leven. Het Leven in relatie tot zijn planetaire omgeving / Earth and Life. Life in relation to its planetary environment*. Dordrecht, Boston, London, Wolters Kluwer Academic Publishers.

Prigogine, Ilya & Stengers, Isabelle
1984   *Order out of Chaos. Man's New Dialogue with Nature.* Toronto etc., Bantam Books.

Primus, Hans
1985a   'Kann Chemie auf Physik reduziert werden? Erster Teil: Das Molekulare Programma.' *Chemie in unserer Zeit 19* 4 (109-119).
1985b   'Kann Chemie auf Physik reduziert werden? Zweiter Teil: Die Chemie der Makrowelt.' *Chemie in unserer Zeit 19* 5 (160-166).

Rathje, William & Murphy, Cullen
1992   *Rubbish! The Archaeology of Garbage. What our garbage tells us about ourselves.* New York, HarperCollins Publishers.

Raup, David M.
1993   *Extinction. Bad Genes or Bad Luck?* Oxford etc., Oxford University Press (1991).

Redman, Ch.L.
1978   *The Rise of Civilization: From Early Farmers to Urban Society in the Ancient Near East.* San Francisco, W.H. Freeman & Co..

Reed, Charles A. (ed.)
1976   *Origins of Agriculture.* The Hague / Paris, Mouton Publishers.

Reeves, Hubert
1981   *Patience dans l'azur: l'evolution cosmique.* Paris, Editions Seuil.

Renfrew, Colin & Bahn, Paul
1991   *Archaeology. Theory, Methods and Practice.* London, Thames & Hudson.

Reynolds, Robert L.
1982   *Europe Emerges. Transition Toward an Industrial World-Wide Society, 600-1750.* Madison, The University of Wisconsin Press (1961).

Roberts, J.M.
1995   *The Penguin History of the World.* London etc. Penguin Books.

Roberts, Neil
1989   *The Holocene. An Environmental History.* Oxford, Basil Blackwell.

Ronan, Colin A. & Needham, Joseph
1986   *The Shorter Science & Civilisation in China: 3. An abridgement by Colin A. Ronan of Joseph Needham's original text.* Cambridge etc., Cambridge University Press.

Rowling, Nick
1987   *Commodities. How the world was taken to market.* London, Free Association Books.

Sanderson, Stephen K.
1995   *Social Transformations. A General Theory of Historical Development.* Oxford, Basil Blackwell.

Saris, Frans W.
1995   'Theorieën van Alles.' (Theories of Everything) *De Gids 153* 5 (May) (407-410).

Scientific American
1994   Special Issue *'Life in the Universe.' 271* 4, October.

Scott, James C.
1995   *State Symplifications. Some Applications to Southeast Asia.* Amsterdam, Centre for Asian Studies Amsterdam, CASA Wertheim lecture 6.

Sherratt, Andrew
1981   'Plough and pastoralism: aspects of the secondary products revolution.' In: Ian Hodder, Glynn Isaac & Norman Hammond (eds.) *Pattern of the Past. Studies in honour of David Clarke.* Cambridge, Cambridge University Press (261-305).

Silk, Joseph
1994   *A Short History of the Universe.* New York etc., W.H. Freeman & Co., Scientific American Library.

Simmons, I.G.
1993   *Environmental History: A Concise Introduction.* Oxford, Basil Blackwell.
1994   *Changing the Face of the Earth. Culture, Environment, History.* Oxford, Basil Blackwell (1989).

Simpson, John & Weiner, Edmund
1989   *Oxford English Dictionary, Second Edition.* Oxford, Clarendon Press.

Smil, Vaclav
1994   *Energy in World History.* Boulder, Colorado, etc., Westview Press.

Smith, Bruce D.
1995   *The Emergence of Agriculture.* New York, W.H. Freeman & Co, Scientific American Library.

Spier, Fred
1990   'Religie in de mensheidsgeschiedenis. Naar een model van de ontwikkeling van religieuze regimes in een lange-termijnperspectief.' (Religion in the History of Humankind. Towards a model of the development of religious regimes in a long-term perspective). *Amsterdams Sociologisch Tijdschrift 16* 4 (88-123).

1992   'Een oud probleem: de relaties tussen mensen en het natuurlijk milieu in een lange termijnperspectief' (An Old Problem: The relations between people and the natural environment in a long-term perspective). *De Gids 150* 2 (96-108).

1994a   *Norbert Elias's Theory of Civilizing Processes Again Under Discussion; An exploration of the sociology of regimes.* Paper for the XIIIth World Congress of Sociology, 18-23 July 1994, Bielefeld, Germany, Ad Hoc Sessions on Figurational Sociology.

1994b   *Religious Regimes in Peru. Religion and state development in a long-term perspective and the effects in the Andean village of Zurite.* Amsterdam, Amsterdam University Press.

1995a   'The Rise and Effectiveness of Dutch Environmental Organisations.' In: Wilma Aarts, Johan Goudsblom, Fred Spier & Kees Schmidt *Toward a Morality of Moderation. Report for the Dutch National Research Programme on Global Air Pollution and Climate Change.* Amsterdam, Amsterdam School for Social Science Research (40-74).

1995b   *San Nicolás de Zurite: Religion and Daily Life of an Andean Village in a Changing World.* Amsterdam, VU University Press.

Stanley, Daniel Jean & Warne, Andrew G.
1993   'Sea level and initiation of Predynastic culture in the Nile delta.' *Nature 363* (435-438).

Stavrianos, Leften
1995   *A Global History. From Prehistory to the Present.* Englewood Cliffs, New Jersey, Prentice-Hall (1971).

1992   *Lifelines From Our Past. A New World History.* Armonk, New York, M.E. Sharp (1989).

Stearns, Peter N.
1993   *The Industrial Revolution in World History.* Boulder, Colorado, etc., Westview Press.

Stewart, Kathlyn
1994   'Early hominid utilisation of fish resources and implications for seasonality and behaviour.' *Journal of Human Evolution 27* (229-245).

110

Swaan, Abram de

1982   *De mens is de mens een zorg* (Who Cares About People). Amsterdam, Meulenhoff.

1985   *Het medisch regiem* (The Medical Regime). Amsterdam, Meulenhoff.

1988   *In Care of the State. Health care, education and welfare in Europe and the USA in the modern era.* New York, Polity Press / Oxford University Press.

1994   *The sociological study of transnational society.* Amsterdam, Amsterdam School for Social Science Research, paper in progress 46.

Taçon, Paul & Chippindale, Christopher

1994   'Australia's Ancient Warriors: Changing Depictions of Fighting in the Rock Art of Arnhem Land, N.T.' *Cambridge Archaeological Journal 4 2* (249-269).

Tattersall, Ian

1993   *The Human Odyssey. Four Million Years of Human Evolution.* New York etc., Prentice Hall.

Trefil, James

1989   *Reading the Mind of God. In Search of the Principle of Universality.* New York, Charles Scribner's Sons.

Trefil, James & Hazen, Robert M.

1995   *The Sciences: An Integrated Approach.* New York etc., John Wiley & Sons Inc.

Tudge, Colin

1993   'Taking the pulse of evolution. Do we owe our existence to short periods of change in the world's climate?' *New Scientist* 24 July (32-36).

Vrba, Elizabeth S.

1993   'Mammal Evolution in the African Neogene and a New Look at the Great American Interchange.' in: Peter Goldblatt (ed.) *Biological Relationships between Africa and South America.* New Haven, London, Yale University Press (393-432).

Vrba, E.S., Partridge, T.C., Denton, G. & Burckle, L.H. (eds.)

1996   *Paleoclimate and evolution with emphasis on human origin.* Yale University Press (forthcoming).

Vree, Wilbert van

1994   *Nederland als vergaderland. Opkomst en uitbreiding van een vergaderregime* (The Netherlands as Assembly Country. The rise and expansion of a meeting regime). Groningen, Wolters-Noordhoff.

Vries, Geert de
1993   *Het pedagogisch regiem* (The Educational Regime). Amsterdam, Meulenhoff.

Wallerstein, Immanuel
1974   *The Modern World-System I. Capitalist Agriculture and the Origins of the European World-Economy in the Sixteenth Century.* New York, Academic Press.
1980   *The Modern World-System II. Mercantilism and the Consolidation of the European World-Economy, 1600-1750.* New York, Academic Press.
1983   *Historical Capitalism.* Londen, Verso.
1989   *The Modern World-System III. The Second Era of Great Expansion of the Capitalist World-Economy, 1730-1840s.* New York, Academic Press.

Weber, Max
1978   *Economy and Society. An outline of interpretive sociology (two volumes).* Berkeley, Los Angeles & London, University of California Press.

Weinberg, Daniela
1978   'Models of Southern Kwakiutl Social Organization.' In: Bruce Cox (ed.) *Cultural Ecology. Readings on the Canadian Indians and Eskimos.* Toronto Ont., The Macmillan Company of Canada (1970).

Weinberg, Steven
1993   *The First Three Minutes. A Modern View of the Origin of the Universe.* London, Flamingo (1977).

Westbroek, Peter
1992   *Life as a Geological Force. Dynamics of the Earth.* New York and London, W.W. Norton & Company (1991).

Williams, M.A.J., Dunkerley, D.L., De Deckker, P., Kershaw, A.P., Stokes, T.
1993   *Quaternary Environments.* London etc., Edward Arnold.

Wilson, Edward O.
1994   *The Diversity of Life.* Harmondsworth, Penguin Books (1992).

Wolf, Eric R.
1982   *Europe and the People Without History*. Berkeley, University of California Press.

Krisciunas, Kevin & Yenne, Bill
1989   *The Pictorial Atlas of the Universe*. Leicester, Magna Books.

Young, Oran R.
1982   *Resource Regimes. Natural Resources and Social Institutions*. Berkeley & Los Angeles, University of California Press.
1986   'International Regimes: Towards a new theory of institutions.' *World Politics 39* 1 (104-122).
1989a   *International Cooperation; Building Regimes for Natural Resources and the Environment*. Ithaca, Cornell University Press.
1989b   'The politics of international regime formation: managing natural resources and the environment.' *International Organization 43* 3 (349-375).